Creative APPLIQUÉ
TO MAKE AND WEAR

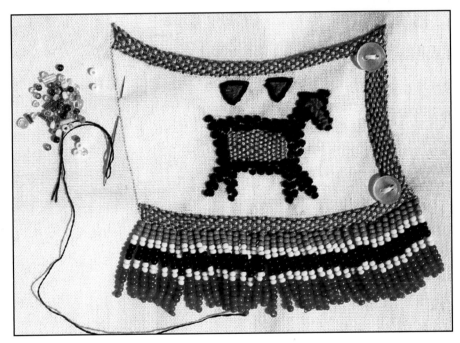

To BJ

Creative
APPLIQUÉ
TO MAKE AND WEAR

LESLEY TURPIN-DELPORT

NEW
HOLLAND

ACKNOWLEDGEMENTS

My thanks to all the pupils of the Lesley Turpin-Delport Studio; the young students from the Art classes and the designers from the Leggats Academy of Design; Neville Anderson and Ronnie Rogoff for photographic assistance; Geoffrey Preston-Thomas and Rachelle Druian.

First published in the United Kingdom in 1989 by
New Holland (Publishers) Ltd
37 Connaught Street
London W2 2AZ

ISBN 1 85368 078 8

Illustrations by Lesley Turpin-Delport and Sue Thompson
Cover The lace work on the cover was embroidered by Jenny Beron
House editor Linda de Villiers
Cover design by Abdul Amien
Design by Jennie Hoare
Layout by Lellyn Creamer

Photosetting by McManus Bros (Pty) Ltd
Reproduction by Adcolour Holdings (Pty) Ltd
Printed and bound in Hong Kong by Leefung-Asco (Pty) Ltd

Whilst every effort has been made to contact the copyright owners of the greetings cards that inspired the appliquéd creations on pages 24 and 106, the publishers would appreciate any information that would enable them to do so.

CONTENTS

INTRODUCTION

Having written two books on the subject of needlecraft (appliqué, embroidery, beading and quilting), where I dealt essentially with techniques and projects, I felt the urge to produce a coffee-table book which would give you, the reader, a glorious visual opportunity to either simply enjoy other people's creativity or to put into practice ideas and techniques incorporating needlecraft and fashion.

The novice can grow with the designs, beginning with simpler images which are added to garments, and then developing the skill of integrating design and third dimension with fashion. Those with more experience will find a wealth of exciting ideas to be interpreted into unique designs incorporating fabric and thread.

My love affair with needlecraft began when I was twelve and it is this passion that I would like to pass onto you, so that you will want to branch out on your own and use your own colour schemes and designs. This book is a sharing of ideas and gives insight into the creative processes that work in my studio. The source materials that excite the students are found all around us — flowers and foliage; figures and faces; children's story books, greetings cards, wrapping paper and calendars; geometric designs and even our heritage. 'Back to the Basics' provides the 'know how' while 'Take the Basics' shows you just how much the various needlecrafts can be enjoyed once you have mastered the basics.

Enthusiasm and a little inspiration are all you need to recreate these beautiful designs.

1 BACK TO THE BASICS

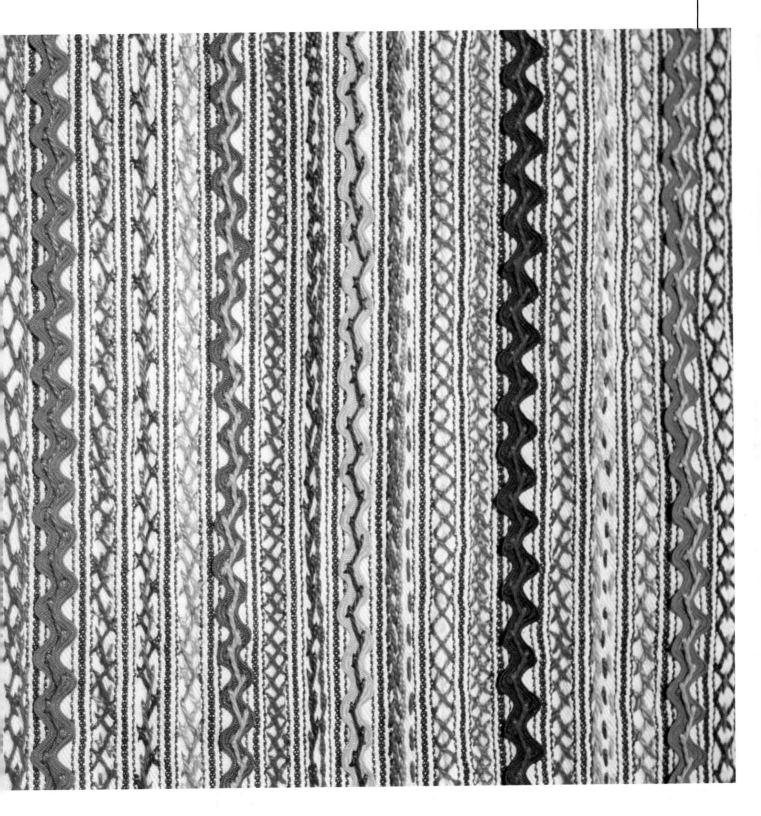

APPLIQUÉ

Appliqué is the name given to the technique of stitching fabric shapes and patches onto an existing or background fabric. This craft has quite practical origins, having been devised to repair worn or holed fabrics with patches. It became more decorative when the patches were cut into shapes and edged with fancy stitches.

Although appliqué is essentially a two-dimensional craft, the textures, stitches and shapes employed in a design provide it with a third dimension. Appliqué is often worked in conjunction with embroidery and quilting, the different craft-forms serving to complement and enhance one another.

The techniques of appliqué described in this book have been kept as simple as possible, but some of the photographs illustrate the degree of complexity and intricacy which can be achieved once the basic elements of this craft have been mastered. How and where the appliqué will be used will determine the design and the colour, which in turn will influence the choice of fabric, thread and stitching technique.

SELECTING AND PREPARING THE FABRICS

Fabric choice will depend on the amount of wear and tear and washing the garment will have to stand up to. Your choice will be further influenced if the appliqué is to be hand- rather than machine-sewn. For hand appliqué, light- and medium-weight fabrics are recommended. Closely woven, natural fabrics such as lawn, chintz, gingham and light-weight wools are best as they are easy to fold. This is only a guide, though, as any fabric can be used if the artist is experienced or particularly talented.

Machine appliqué allows a far larger fabric choice because no fold-over seam allowance is necessary, unlike the hand method which requires that seams be folded over and stitched (thus creating more bulk).

Fine fabrics like silk, dacron, tulle and lace, as well as coarse, heavier fabrics, such as denim, corduroy, velvet, leather and suede, can be used. However, when working with garments, it is advisable to choose appliqué fabrics with the same weight and durability as the garment. It is also wise to pre-shrink the fabrics and to check that they are colourfast before use.

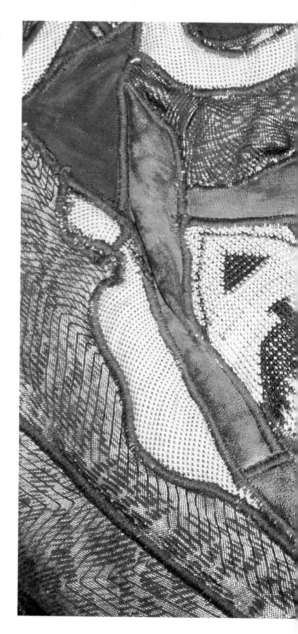

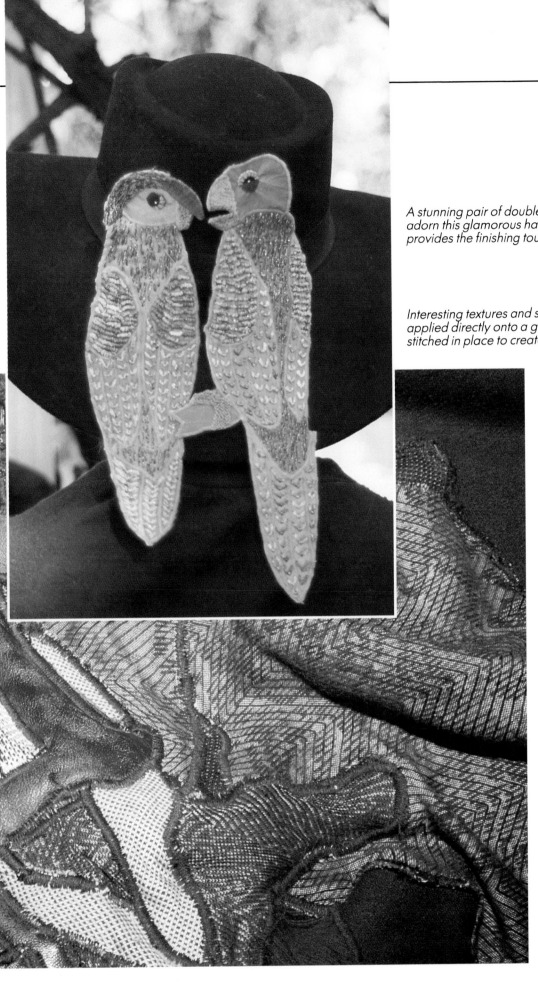

A stunning pair of double fabric appliqués adorn this glamorous hat. Rich embroidery provides the finishing touch.

Interesting textures and shapes can be applied directly onto a garment and satin stitched in place to create a new fabric.

PLANNING THE DESIGN

COLOUR choice is personal, but there are definite colour principles which you can employ when planning your designs.

COMPLEMENTARY COLOURS (opposite colours on the colour wheel) red/green, yellow/purple and orange/blue, create a visual vibrancy.

PRIMARY COLOURS: blue, yellow and red will dominate a design because they are pure colours.

JUXTAPOSED COLOURS (those that lie next to each other on the colour wheel): blue, green and violet for example, blend together softly.

TONES are colours mixed with grey and are ideal for shadow areas because of their subdued nature.

TINTS are colours mixed with white and are excellent for highlighting.

NEUTRAL COLOURS: black, white and grey work well with any colour.

PATTERN AND TEXTURE The correct choice of pattern and the texture of the fabric is vital to the success of a design. For example, geometric fabrics create optical illusions while granny prints add charm, and textured fabrics an extra dimension.

ENLARGING THE DESIGN

Should you wish to enlarge your chosen design, first trace it onto a sheet of tracing paper. Place the tracing paper over some graph paper so that you have a squared-up drawing, or use a ruler and a felt tip pen to make an evenly squared grid on top of the design (use the graph paper as a guide). Now, on a clean sheet of paper, draw another grid the size you require for the eventual design. The second grid must have the same number of squares as the original.

Copy the design, square by square, onto the larger grid, referring to the corresponding squares on the original grid. It helps to number the squares on both grids.

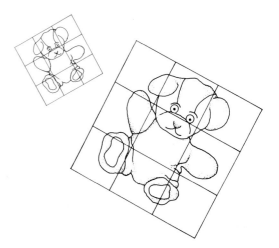

An example of direct appliqué with the charming touch of using eyelets and real laces.

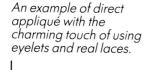

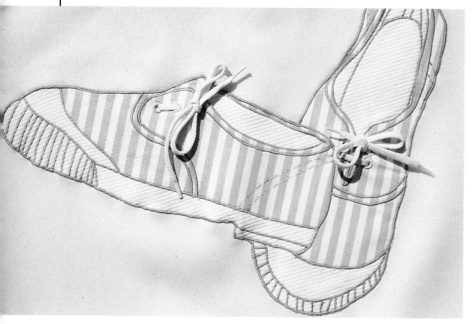

NOTE If the design is complicated, make a tracing from your enlarged design and, when assembling the appliquéd shapes on the background, lay the tracing on top to ensure that all the pieces are correctly positioned. Should the design consist of many pieces, it may help to number the pieces on the drawing.

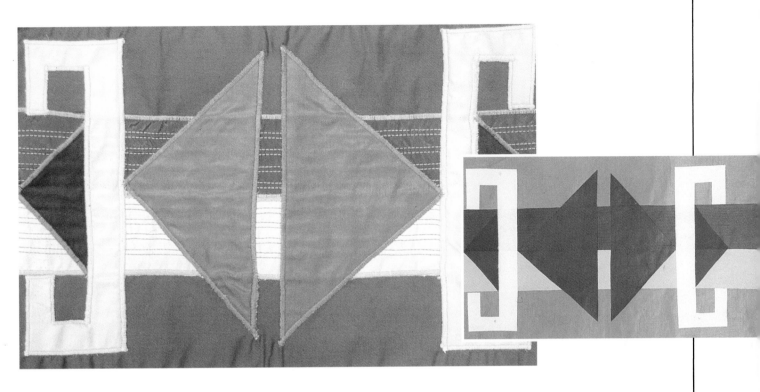

TRANSFERRING THE DESIGN

There are several ways to transfer designs onto your background fabric:

IRON-ON VILENE is a transparent, bonded interfacing that is ideal for appliqué because it can be placed over the original drawing and the shapes in the design traced onto it. These shapes are then cut out, ironed onto the appliqué fabric and used as a pattern for cutting out the fabric shapes.

The vilene backing strengthens the shapes and prevents unravelling. Vilene is available in different thicknesses and should be chosen according to the fabric you are working with (single-layered appliqué shapes require a thicker vilene than do multi-layered shapes).

APPLIQUÉ PAPER For simple appliqué designs, the design is drawn onto the smooth side of this paper and then cut out. This piece is then ironed, rough side down, onto the 'wrong' side of the fabric to be used for the design; the fabric is cut around the design and the paper peeled off the back leaving an adhesive web of vilene. The appliqué piece is then placed in position on the fabric or garment and ironed again. The design is now firmly fixed

in place and can now be stitched on your sewing machine, using a closed zigzag.

TEMPLATES can be made if the design is simple or repetitive. Make the templates from cardboard or old X-ray plates, then place them directly on the fabric and cut around them.

DRESSMAKER'S CARBON AND TRACING WHEEL are also suitable. Place the carbon between the fabric and the design, and run the wheel along the design lines with enough pressure to transfer the design onto the fabric.

A HOT TRANSFER PENCIL is excellent for marking designs on garments where the lines can be covered with fabric paint or beads.

A SECOND DRAWING can be made and cut up into pieces. Place the pattern pieces on the right side of the fabric, draw around them and cut them out, leaving a 5 mm seam allowance around each piece where necessary.

A DRESSMAKER'S PENCIL or a very light pencil can be used to trace designs directly onto sheer (transparent) fabrics.

These two designs have been prepared with appliqué paper. An ideal choice for transferring the design because the shapes are simple and easily defined.

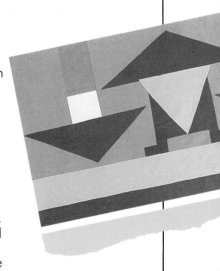

Tiny pieces of fabric have been hand appliquéd and then trimmed with embroidery touches.

HAND APPLIQUÉ

To transfer your design onto fabric, I find the iron-on vilene method the most successful. As vilene is available in different thicknesses, choose the correct weight for your design. For example, if your design consists of a single layer of fabric, use a fairly thick vilene, but if it is made up of multiple layers, use a finer vilene.

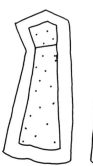

Design to be appliquéd

Place the vilene, shiny side up, over the design. Trace each shape separately, using a soft pencil. Overlapping shapes must be drawn as though they were uninterrupted. It is not necessary to add seam allowances to the vilene.

Cut out the vilene pieces and place them, shiny side down, onto the wrong side of the fabric, leaving at least 10 mm between each shape for the fabric seam allowance.

Iron on the vilene and cut out the fabric shapes leaving a 5 mm seam allowance of fabric around each vilene shape.

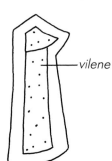

vilene

fabric

Begin the hand appliqué by turning under the seam allowances. Fold the fabric at the edge of the vilene and tack along the fold around each piece.

This design is a wonderful example of hand appliqué and stuffed shapes. The details are embroidered with one strand of embroidery thread and the illusion of fabric and beads is quite stunning.

Curved edges must be clipped and notched to make a perfect shape.

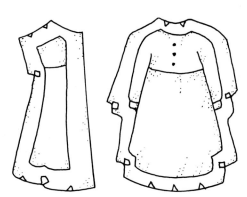

Corners can be turned and folded (like a parcel) or mitred to give good points.

Corners (parcel fold)

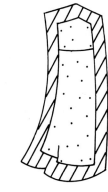
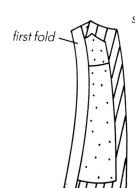

first fold   second fold

Corners (mitre fold)

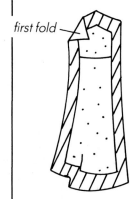

first fold

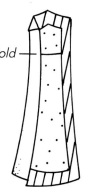

second fold

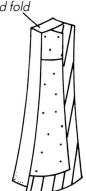

third fold

Once the seam allowance has been turned under and tacked, attach the shapes to the background fabric.

Single shapes can be attached by using any of the variety of stitches described opposite.

Multiple shapes can be whip stitched (see opposite) together first and then attached to the background. An alternative method is to lap the top shape over the lower shape's raw edge.

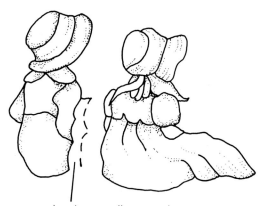

raw edge (seam allowance)

Another method of assembling hand appliqué is to fold the seam allowances under, pin the shape directly onto the background and stitch the shape in place. This method is ideal if the shapes are going to be stuffed. A few appliqué stitches are made, the stuffing is tucked into place and the stitching is then completed.

HAND APPLIQUÉ STITCHES Tiny whip stitches, running stitches, blind hem stitches and back stitch, as well as a variety of decorative embroidery stitches, are all suitable for securing hand appliquéd designs to the background fabric. Back stitch and whip stitch give a flat edge and are very secure while blind hemming gives a soft rounded edge.

BLIND HEM STITCH These stitches should be almost invisible. Bring the needle through the fold of the seam allowance and pick up a few threads of the ground

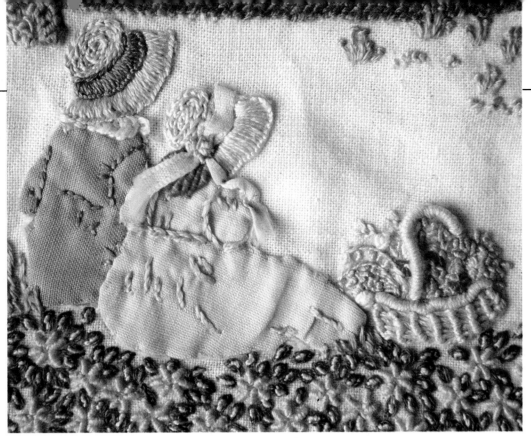

These lilliputian figures are no larger than your thumb. These are hand appliqués given definition with embroidery stitches.

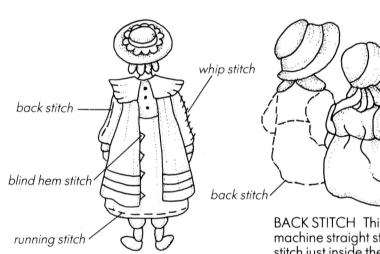

back stitch
whip stitch
blind hem stitch
running stitch

back stitch
blind hem stitch

running stitch
whip stitch

fabric. Re-insert the needle through the fold and slide it along the fold for about 5 mm. Bring the needle through the fold and pick up a few threads of background fabric. Continue in this way around the appliqué shape.

RUNNING STITCH Weave the needle in and out of the fabric just inside the folded edge of the appliqué, making tiny running stitches through both the appliqué and the background fabric.

WHIP STITCH Bring the needle up through the appliqué a short distance from the edge and re-insert it into the background at the edge of the appliqué, making a small diagonal stitch. Continue stitching, maintaining the diagonal.

BACK STITCH This stitch resembles machine straight stitching. Make a small stitch just inside the folded edge of the appliqué. Leave a small space and come up the same distance away as the length of the first stitch. Re-insert the needle at the end of the first stitch, thus making a small back stitch.

Shapes can also be hand embroidered to the background using a selection of embroidery stitches. This method is both decorative and functional (see pages 26-33). Embroidery defines the outlines of the shapes and is a particularly good method for attaching stuffed or quilted shapes to the background fabric.

Tiny pieces of appliqué with a raw edge (i.e. with no fold-over seam allowance) can be attached with embroidery stitches, as long as the raw edges are completely covered by the embroidery work.

MACHINE APPLIQUÉ

Machine appliqué is stronger and faster to carry out than hand appliqué. The raw edges around the cut out shapes are not folded over and tacked, but are covered with a closed zigzag stitch. A closed zigzag setting creates a definite, ridged satin stitch, while a slightly open setting creates a more zigzag-like pattern. A fairly narrow stitch-width setting (approximately 2 on most machines) combined with a close zigzag setting (approximately ½) is suitable for most work. Bobbin tension can be made a little tighter than usual, as this will pull the top threads through to give a well-rounded satin stitch. Good quality thread must be used to achieve a smooth, satiny finish.

The colour choice of thread will depend on whether the design requires delineation, in which case a contrasting thread is preferable, or whether the colour zones are sufficiently marked, in which case a matching thread is best.

DIRECT APPLIQUÉ

This method is suitable for designs that are neither too large nor complex. Prepare the shapes by using the following iron-on vilene technique:

1. Place the vilene, shiny side up, over the design and trace each shape separately using a soft pencil. Draw all the details onto each piece.

2. Where two raw edges will meet, an *underlap seam allowance* of 5 mm must be marked on one piece of the vilene. This will be tucked under the adjacent piece when

assembled. An underlap seam allowance is only added to a piece that will not change the design when the shapes are assembled. Superimposed pieces do not require underlap allowances.

3. Cut out the pieces along the marked outlines.

4. Iron the vilene shapes, shiny side down, onto the wrong side of the fabric. Remember the straight grain of the appliqué shape must run in the same direction as the straight grain of the background fabric so as to prevent puckering and stretching.

5. Cut out the fabric shapes following the vilene outlines (no seam allowances necessary). The shapes are now ready to assemble.

6. Place the shapes *directly* onto the background fabric and tack in position. Using machine thread, tack close to the edge of the design so that the zigzag stitch (step 7) will cover the tacking. A glue stick can be used to secure small pieces before machining.

7. To secure the thread before zigzagging, set the machine on straight stitch, with the width on (0) and the length on (0). Make a few stitches - this knots the threads together. (End your work in the same manner.) Now change the stitch width to 2 and the zigzag to ½ and machine stitch, working from the centre of the design outwards. Be sure that the needle is very sharp, and check that it enters the fabric from the raw edge inwards.

8. At a corner, leave the needle in the fabric on the outside of the line of stitches, lift the foot, then turn the fabric and continue stitching so that the next stitch overlaps the previous stitch.

Horizontals balanced by strong verticals.

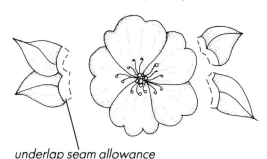

underlap seam allowance

Direct appliqué leaves and petals in chintz with free-form petals for added dimension.

DOUBLE VILENE TECHNIQUE

This is a technique suitable for designs that are too large to pass comfortably through a machine, for example quilts; shapes that are going to be heavily embroidered or beaded; and for designs on garments such as T-shirts and jackets. The shapes are machine stitched first and then attached to the background fabric by hand or machine. A slightly raised effect is also an interesting aspect of this technique.

3. Iron the vilene shapes, shiny side down, onto the wrong side of the appliqué fabric.

1. With the vilene shiny side up, trace the shapes in the design onto the vilene using a soft pencil. Add an underlap seam allowance where two raw edges will meet. Superimposed pieces do not require an underlap allowance.

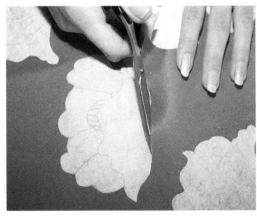

4. Cut out the fabric shapes following the vilene outlines. Now the *second* piece of vilene is used – hence the name 'double vilene technique'.

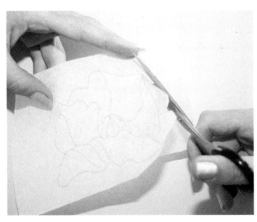

2. Cut out the vilene shapes on your marked outlines.

5. Assemble the shapes according to your design onto another piece of iron-on or ordinary vilene. The vilene must be large enough to protrude all around the edges of the design. Superimpose and underlap where necessary. Tack or glue the pieces in position. If iron-on vilene is used, tack or glue the pieces onto the *dull* side.

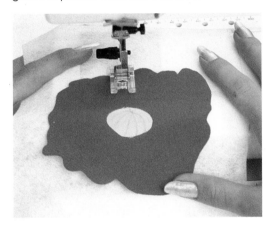

6. Place the design in the machine and satin stitch all the raw edges.

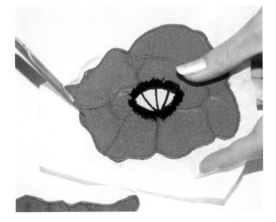

7. Carefully cut away the excess vilene without cutting into the zigzag stitching. If necessary embellish the design as required with embroidery, beading or decorative stitching.

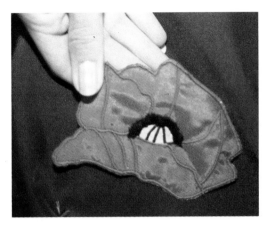

8. Place the design onto the background fabric and secure it by hand, using the same colour thread and a small blind hem stitch (page 16) over the satin-stitched edge. Alternatively it can be secured by machine with an open zigzag over the satin-stitched edge. A straight stitch just inside the overlocked edge is also suitable. If iron-on vilene is used, the design can be ironed, instead of tacked, onto the background, provided the design is not beaded or heavily embroidered.

The double vilene technique has been used to make these flowers. The centres of these machine appliquéd silk poppies are looping foot coils.

This double fabric appliqué has been wired with fine florist wire to give the wings the 'lift off' effect.

DOUBLE FABRIC TECHNIQUE

This is an extension of the double vilene technique and is used when three-dimensional shapes or reversible free-form images are required.

Follow the steps for the Double Vilene Technique but, instead of using the second piece of vilene as backing, place the shapes on the wrong side of a second piece of fabric.

Proceed as for the previous technique, satin stitching the shape and cutting away the excess fabric. These shapes can be stuffed very successfully.

FREE-FORM PETALS

Free-form petals are made by stitching two shapes together, turning through and then attaching to the appliqué.

1. Cut out double petals. With right sides together, machine straight stitch the shapes together, leaving a small opening for turning through.

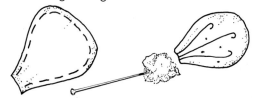

2. Trim the seam allowance, clip any curves and turn through. Now lightly stuff the shapes.

Top quilting can be added to give the petals definition.

3. Attach the petals to the background and satin stitch in place, closing the opening at the same time. Alternatively, hand hem or embroider the petals in position.

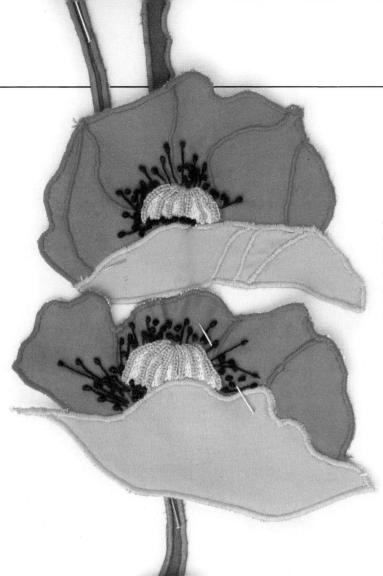

Appliquéd poppies, pinned in position so they protrude from a pocket, can be straight stitched or hand hemmed in place. The centres are worked in buttonhole bars and extended French knots.

Five apricot double fabric appliqué petals strung together and attached to a stuffed centre make ideal appliqués for shoulder pad and belt decoration.

THREE DIMENSIONAL PETALS

These petals are usually made from suede or soft leather. *If leather is not used*, make the petals using the Double Fabric Technique, as previously described.

1. Cut out five petals and a circle for the centre of the flower. Take a double thread and string the five petals onto it. Pull up the thread tightly, gathering the petals to form a circle. End off with a strong back stitch.

2. Run a gathering thread around the edge of the suede or leather circle and pull up, inserting a piece of wadding as you tighten the circle so that it resembles a stuffed button. Attach the ring of petals to the back of the stuffed centre with whip stitches. Decorate the centre with beads if desired.

3. A small piece of Velcro can be stitched to the back of the flower and to the garment so that the flower can be removed before washing.

EMBROIDERY

Embroidery is one of the most versatile yet unexplored handcrafts known to man. A knowledge of basic embroidery stitches combined with a creative imagination provides the designer with a means of self expression. Embroidery is like painting with thread.

BASIC REQUIREMENTS

Before you begin, make sure that you have the following basic equipment:

Needles (A good selection of very sharp to blunt-tipped needles [for wool or weaving] is essential.)
Scissors (Small, sharp-pointed)
Thimble for leather work.
Thread (It is handy to have different types of embroidery thread. There is an excellent selection available: six-strand cotton, coton perlé, crewel wool, metallic thread, crochet cotton and new textured wools to mention just a few.)
Beeswax to prevent knots and tangles

Embroidery ring to keep the ground fabric taut while the embroidery is being worked.
Fabrics (Any fabric is suitable for decorative embroidery. The appliqué background will dictate your choice of thread and stitch technique.)

TRANSFERRING THE DESIGN

There are a number of methods of transferring a design onto fabric:

IRON-ON VILENE is invaluable for the crafts person who cannot draw well. Place the vilene, *shiny side down*, onto the design. Trace the design onto the vilene, cut out the shape and iron it directly onto the appliqué. By the time the design is complete, the vilene will not be noticeable.

TRACING PAPER Use masking tape to attach your design to a windowpane. Place a piece of tracing paper over it and trace the outlines with a pencil. Go over the design on the reverse side of the tracing paper, place this against your fabric and draw over it with enough pressure to transfer the design onto the fabric.

HOT TRANSFER PENCIL Trace the design onto tracing paper and go over the back of the design with a hot transfer pencil. Iron the design onto the fabric.

TRACING DIRECTLY FROM A DRAWING This can be done if the fabric is transparent. Place the fabric over the design and trace over the outlines with a pencil. Use dressmaker's pencils in pink, blue or white or use a fabric pen which washes out or fades after 24 hours.

DRESSMAKER'S CARBON Trace the design onto tracing paper. Place the dressmaker's carbon face down between the background fabric and the tracing. Go over the outlines to transfer the design.

The inspiration for this design was a delightful greetings card. It combines a number of techniques and the attention to detail is marvellous- especially the little snail with the parcel on its back.

This glorious basket of flowers grew out of a clever combination of traditional stitches. The added dimension is achieved by creating a textile sandwich (top layer, batting (wadding) and lining, see page 40) and by echo quilting the basic outline. Fine embroidery thread gives a delicate interpretation, while the use of tapestry wools would be bold and dynamic.

HAND EMBROIDERY

The rich jewel-like colours are intensified by the clustering of flowers and the dense handling of the background leaves worked in French knots, Roumanian stitch, lazy daisy and bullion knots.

Most fine embroidery is worked using two strands of six-strand embroidery thread. Bullion knots and French knots work well with three strands while grub knot roses require all six strands. For bold effects, use many strands of embroidery thread or wool yarn but do use thread that is compatible with your background fabric i.e. silk on silk, cotton on cotton and so on.

Cut your threads about 20 cm long and wax them, if necessary, to prevent tangles and knots. Begin and end with a back stitch and not a knot.

USEFUL EMBROIDERY STITCHES

The stitches described below are the ones I find particularly useful for details on an appliqué design.

STEM STITCH Work from the left to the right, keeping the thread to the left of the needle and making small, even stitches. By repeating this stitch you can fill an area. When stem stitch is used to attach an appliqué design, it is often referred to as outline stitch.

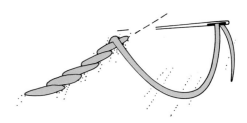

BACK STITCH Bring the thread through the fabric and make a small stitch backwards. Then take the needle forwards under the fabric and come out one stitch length ahead, ready for the next stitch backwards. Keep all the stitches the same length. This stitch is ideal for facial outlines on appliqué designs.

WHIPPED BACK STITCH This stitch gives a heavier line than ordinary back stitch. Begin by working a foundation row of back stitches slightly longer than usual, and then whip a second thread over the line, without picking up any background fabric; use a blunt-ended needle for the whipping to avoid splitting the foundation thread.

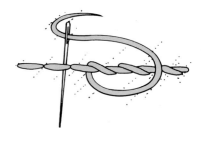

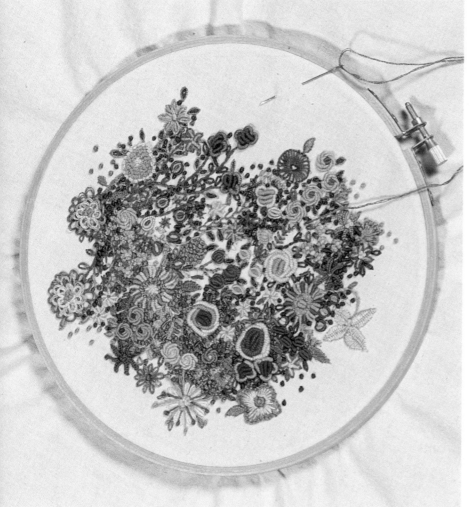

WOVEN BACK STITCH Begin by working a foundation row of back stitch. Without picking up any background fabric, weave in and out of the back stitch, leaving a small loop each side of the back stitch.

BUTTONHOLE BAR Make two or three parallel stitches across a space and secure with a small stitch. Now form buttonhole stitches around the loose strands without picking up the background fabric.

This design includes almost every technique described in this book - the little dress is appliqué, the face is trapunto quilting and the surrounding details are exquisite embroidery.

BUTTONHOLE STITCH This is an excellent stitch for decorative hand appliqué or patchwork because it is so versatile. The stitches can be worked close together (blanket stitch) or open or radiating to form a circle. It can also be used to create buttonhole bars and scalloped edges.

Bring the needle through the fabric. Insert the needle above and to the right of the first stitch, and come out parallel to the bottom of the first stitch with the thread held under the needle. Pull through downwards.

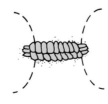

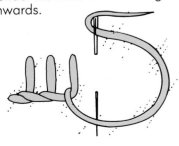

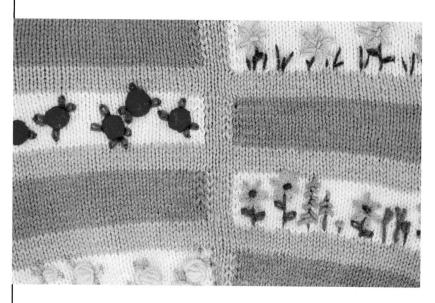

WHIPPED CHAIN STITCH Work a foundation row of chain stitch first and then whip at regular intervals with a second thread (do not pick up any background fabric). Use a blunt-ended tapestry needle for the whipping to avoid splitting the stitches on the foundation row.

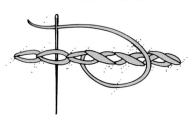

RAISED CHAIN STITCH This is a difficult combination stitch. Work a ladder of parallel stitches approximately 3 mm apart. Bring the thread through the fabric at the beginning of the ladder. Pass the thread over and under the first strand. Pull through, keeping the thread taut. With the thread to the left, make a loop by passing downwards under the same strand, to the right of the first stitch, and over the thread of the loop. Do not pull too tightly. Continue making the chains along the ladder. If the bar is wide, several rows of raised chain can be worked. Always start at the top.

Grub knot roses and lazy daisies are embroidered in fine wool onto a handmade child's jersey.

CHAIN STITCH Bring the thread through the fabric. Hold the thread to the left making a loop shape. Re-insert the needle at the starting point, bring it out again a short distance away and take it over the loop of the thread. Pull through. Repeat the loop, inserting the needle exactly where the thread came out, inside the previous loop. Chain stitch can be used as a filler if it is worked in continuous rows. Always work in one direction, beginning each new row at the same end.

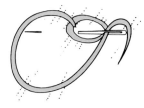

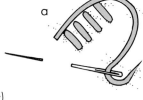

a

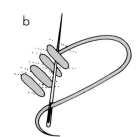

b

DETACHED CHAIN STITCH (Lazy daisy) Work a single chain stitch and anchor it with a small straight stitch. Five small, detached chain stitches arranged like a flower make a daisy – hence the name.

c

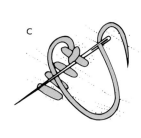

d

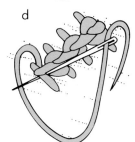

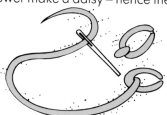

SATIN STITCH This stitch looks easy but it takes practice to make it perfect. The stitches should fit closely together with very smooth and straight outside edges. The stitch may be straight or slanted. For large areas use a long and short satin stitch for delicate shading.

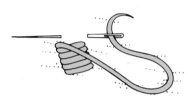

LONG AND SHORT SATIN STITCH The outline of the shape can be marked with split stitch, chain or even a small running stitch. Work the first row of long and short satin stitches, following the outline of the shape. In the following rows all the stitches will be of equal length. For a shaded effect use a thread which is slightly lighter or darker.

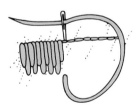

ROUMANIAN STITCH This is a satin stitch held down with a smaller slanting stitch in the centre. The stitches can be worked either very closely together or further apart.

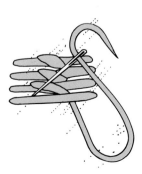

COUCHING This technique can be used in linear work or as a solid filling. Threads are laid down on the surface of the fabric and are held in place with another thread. Any type of thread may be couched.

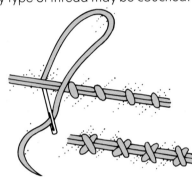

Contrasting colours may be used and many different holding stitches are suitable, including cross stitch, herring bone, straight stitch, fly stitch and detached chain. When couching in a circle, try to create a rhythm with the holding stitches by controlling the pattern made by the stitches.

Two- and three-strand embroidery in pastel shades. Play with the basic embroidery stitches and see how many different flowers you can make using clever combinations.

SPLIT STITCH This stitch is made using an even number of strands. Make a single straight stitch. Now bring the needle back up between the strands, piercing through the centre of the stitch from below, dividing the strands exactly in the middle.

Repeat, forming a neat line of stitches. I find this stitch particularly good for filling in large areas. In order to achieve a smooth finish, stagger the splits by making the split a little past or a little short of the split in the previous row.

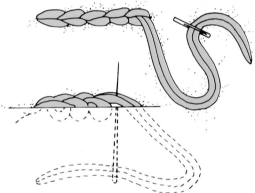

FLY STITCH Work a straight stitch but come up in the centre of the stitch at a diagonal. Pull through and anchor the stitch with a small tying stitch. Fly stitch can be spaced evenly or scattered at random over a shape. The tying stitch can vary in length to produce different effects.

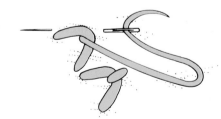

Different wools, silk and beads have been combined to create a fabric which resembles a beautiful tapestry. Traditional embroidery stitches are the basic techniques used here.

FEATHER STITCH Work a single feather stitch. The base of the first stitch forms the branch of the second stitch. Work a stitch to the left on the same level and then to the right. Continue working these two movements alternately.

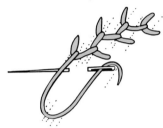

LAID WORK This lattice stitch is very similar to couching. It is used as a stabilizing factor over large areas of satin stitch. Make parallel slanting lines over the satin stitch in the opposite direction. Cover the whole area in this way, and then work lines in the opposite direction, thus forming diamond shapes. Tie these threads down with a small stitch at each intersection.

FRENCH KNOT Bring the needle through the fabric. Hold the thread taut with the left hand while wrapping the thread around the needle one or two times. Re-insert the needle close to where the thread emerged. French knots can be scattered like little seeds or used to fill an area. They are ideal for flower centres.

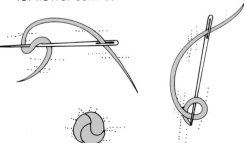

EXTENDED FRENCH KNOT Bring the needle through the fabric. Hold the thread taut and place the needle across the thread a small distance away from the exit point. Wrap the thread around the needle one or two times. Keeping the 'stalk' taut, re-insert the needle at this point. The length of the 'stalk' can vary, if desired.

COLONIAL KNOT Pull the thread through the fabric. Place the needle under the thread, sliding the needle from left to right (a). Wrap the thread over the top of the needle from right to left creating a figure eight (b). Insert the needle into the fabric close to where it emerged; pull the working thread taut with your left hand so that a firm, tight knot is formed (c). Pull the needle to the wrong side of the fabric forming a colonial knot. Come up at the next dot (d).

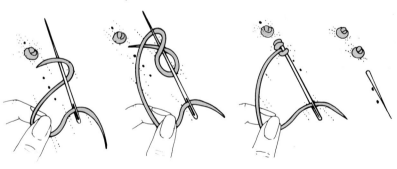

NOTE If you are left handed, reverse the procedure as shown.

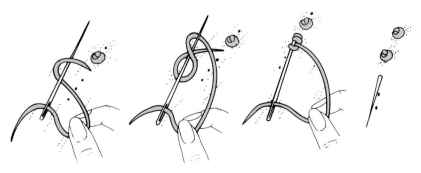

The face is worked in split stitch using fine grey wool. The finer details are embroidered into the split stitch using three strands of embroidery thread.

BULLION KNOT The bullion knot is a long 'sausage-shaped' knot. Bring a small-eyed needle through the fabric. Pick up the fabric the distance required for the bullion knot but do not pull the needle through. Twist the thread several times around the needle. Holding the coils on the needle with your thumb, pull the thread through and insert the needle at the starting point to anchor the bullion knot. These knots may be worked individually or in rows or in a combination to form a rosebud.

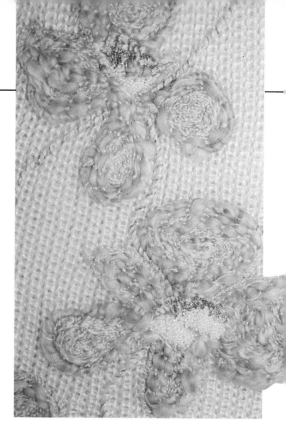

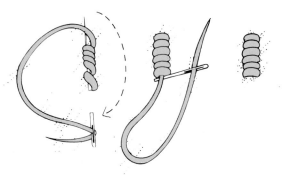

Floral source material is the key to simple designing. Chunky wools are couched onto the garment and the centres decorated in French knots and bullions.

BULLION ROSEBUD Work a small six-twist bullion knot. Then work an eight-twist bullion knot on each side of the first bullion knot. This size rosebud is ideal for smocking decoration, but the size can be increased by adding successive bullion knots with increasing numbers of twists on each side.

GRUB KNOT ROSE This rose is made of bullion knots using six strands of thread and 11 twists throughout. Make three parallel raised bullion knots, then work around these with four bullion knots, slightly overlapping each other. Continue with five bullion knots and finish with seven. Colour changes can be made by starting with the darkest colour in the centre.

LOOPED BULLION KNOT Work four bullion loops by working 20-twist bullion knots with the point of return as close as possible to the point of entry. Then work three to four loops in the space between the first four loops. The loops must look intertwined.

WOVEN SPIDER'S WEB Work a foundation of spokes first; these should be of an odd number and should radiate from the central point of the circle. Now weave a second thread under and over the spokes, beginning at the centre and working outwards; be careful not to pick up any ground fabric. Use a blunt-ended tapestry needle for the second thread to avoid splitting the foundation stitches. The second thread can be of a contrasting colour and a round thread, such as pearl cotton, makes the spider's web stand out more from the background than a flat, stranded thread.

A woven spider's web made with an even number of spokes gives a totally different effect, resembling a catherine wheel.

WHIPPED SPIDER'S WEB Make two crosses creating eight spokes. Bring the needle up in the centre of the spokes and pull through. Using a blunt needle, wrap the thread around the spoke just behind the exit thread, slide the needle under that spoke and the next one, i.e. the needle goes back around one and under two spokes until all the spokes are covered.

Work tightly in the centre to accent the whipped spokes, allowing the threads to become slightly looser towards the outer edge. Colour changes can be made. The spokes can be covered completely or the centre can be worked leaving part of the spokes showing. Any size can be made and tiny spider's webs look just like daisies.

PEKINESE STITCH This is another decorative weaving stitch. Make a foundation row of back stitches and then, using a blunt-ended tapestry needle and working from the left, weave through the back stitches to form a braid-like effect. You can use the same colour or a contrast thread. This stitch worked in concentric circles, starting from the outside and working inwards, makes a beautiful daisy.

A basic geometric design where the student has explored the potential of basic embroidery stitches combined with trapunto quilting.

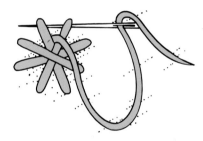

WEAVING STITCH This stitch is very effective if you want to create the illusion of a basket weave. Make a series of long stitches, side by side, the width of one thread apart. With a blunt needle and using a contrast thread, weave over and under the threads, starting at the widest part. Push the threads together as each line is worked so that even squares of each colour appear.

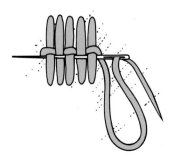

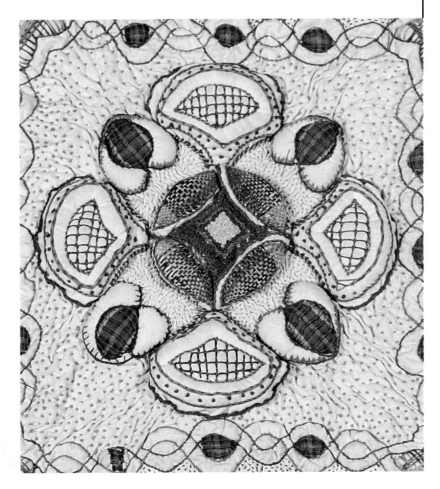

WORKING WITH WOOL AND BRAID

All the embroidery stitches illustrated on pages 26-33 can also be worked in wool to create exciting added dimensions to your work. Traditional embroidery stitches worked in wool instead of embroidery thread give a tapestry-like effect. When using 'chunky' wools, it is best to use couching or any of the woven stitches. Embroidery worked on this scale is quick and easy and the effect dynamic.

WOOLLEN LOOPS can be used to create hair. One method is to bend a wire hanger into a U-shape and then wind the wool around the wire as shown. Machine straight stitch along the middle of the wool, sliding the woollen loops off the hanger as

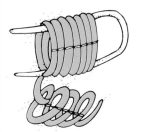

you proceed. These loops can then be stitched onto the appliqué.

Another method of making loops is with a metal looping foot. Set the machine as for appliqué satin stitch (zigzag with a stitch width of about 2 and a stitch length of about ½). When turning corners, lift the needle out of the fabric, raise the presser bar and push the loops off the metal shaft. Swivel the fabric, lower the presser bar and continue looping. The looping must be manually knotted on completion.

BRAID Silk hair can be created by pulling off coils of a silk dressing gown cord to make ideal ringlets. Attach the coils by couching them onto the appliqué.

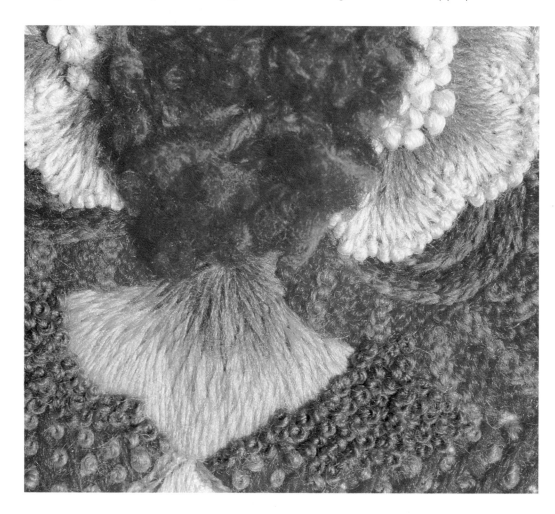

This detail of the exotic flower illustrates a sensitive choice of embroidery stitches, which range from laid work filled with French knots, raised chain stitch and split stitch to a French knotted and tufted centre.

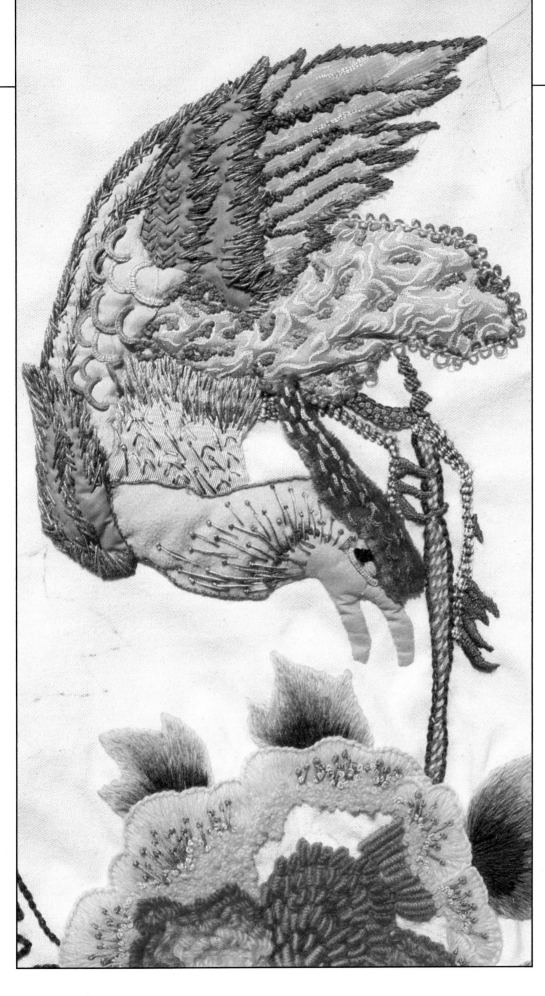

This exotic bird illustrates the wonderful effect achieved when exciting embroidery stitches are used to attach the hand appliqué to the background. An impression of depth is created by stuffing the shapes lightly as the areas are closed. Notice the subtle colour change and use of mixed threads. A good choice of appliqué fabric enhances the whole design.

BEADS AND SEQUINS

Bugle and seed beads are worked onto a stiffened organza base.

These plimsolls have been hand painted with fabric paint and decorated with rhine-stones and bright blue ribbons instead of laces.

*B*eads and sequins can add glamour and dazzle to appliquéd garments. The selection of beads available is fantastic, ranging from tiny glass beads, rhinestones and clay beads to carved, wooden beads. For appliqué, I recommend the following basic types:

Tiny glass beads in a variety of colours, both opaque and transparent
Bugle beads, in various lengths and colours
Sequins in different shapes and sizes

BEADS should be placed neatly together in a pre-arranged order. A very long, thin needle with a tiny eye is a must. Choose the thread colour to suit your article and use a double thread, beginning and ending with a knot and a back stitch for extra strength.

INDIVIDUAL BEADS To attach individual beads, bring the needle through the fabric, thread the bead onto it and pull through. Insert the needle next to the first exit and make a stitch slightly longer than the bead, keeping the thread below the needle as illustrated. Pull through.

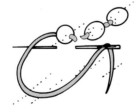

Individual large beads can also be attached with a tiny seed bead as shown.

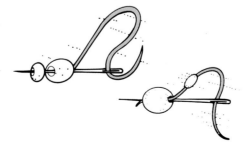

SEEDING (Crusting) Bring the needle through the fabric and thread on three tiny beads. Re-insert the needle into the fabric so that centre bead rests on top of the other two.

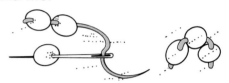

COUCHING BEADS Bring the needle through the fabric, thread a number of beads onto the needle and pull the thread through. Position the first bead on the ground fabric and, with a separate needle and thread, make a holding stitch, close to the bead, over the first thread. Slide the second bead up to the first and continue couching the thread between each bead.

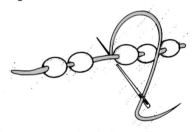

An alternative method of couching is to thread a number of beads onto the thread (like a necklace). Anchor this string of beads at the end with a back stitch. Position the 'necklace' on your design, then come back over it, catching the thread down between every second or third bead.

DANGLING BEADS Secure the thread to the ground fabric and thread three bugle beads and one tiny bead onto it. Re-insert the needle through the bugle beads using the tiny bead as the anchor. Secure the thread to the background. The length of each 'chain' can be varied, depending on the number of bugle beads used.

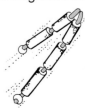

SEQUINS There are a number of different methods of attaching sequins. Here are four examples:

SINGLE BACK STITCH Bring the needle through the fabric and sequin. Hold the sequin in position and make a back stitch over the right side of it. Bring the needle up again to the left side of the sequin, leaving enough space for the next sequin to fit edge to edge with the first.

DOUBLE BACK STITCH Bring the thread through the fabric and sequin. Make a back stitch over the right side of the sequin, then bring the needle out to the left of the sequin and make a second back stitch through the eye of the sequin. Bring the needle through the fabric, leaving sufficient space for the next sequin.

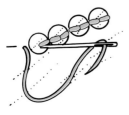

SEQUINS WITH BEADS Bring the needle through the fabric and sequin. Thread a tiny seed bead onto the needle and reinsert the needle through the eye of the sequin, pulling the thread tightly so that the tiny bead secures the sequin to the fabric.

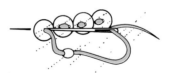

INVISIBLE SEQUIN STITCH Bring the needle through the fabric and sequin. Make a small stitch to the left, over the sequin and into the fabric. Come back through the fabric, leaving a small space half the size of a sequin. Thread on the second sequin and once again make a small stitch to the left, over the sequin and into the fabric. The second sequin must overlap the first so that the rim covers the thread and the eye of the previous sequin.

Minute beads arranged to resemble petit point. This beautiful example of beadwork was made by my great-grandmother.

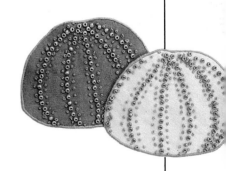

Embroidery and beadwork combine perfectly to decorate these appliqué shells.

Sequins and tiny beads reinforce the flower design.

Pearls and sequins give an enchanting chiaroscuro to the lace appliqué on the bodice of this bride's gown.

Be adventurous and combine an assortment of beads and sequins to create different effects.

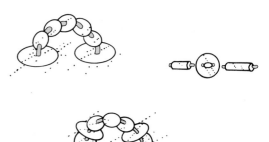

Appliqué given a lift with white-on-white beading. The leaf detail is chain stitch with tiny pearls.

These examples illustrate the wonderful combinations possible with clever beadwork. Embroidery is an excellent base for a subtle effect.

BEADS AND EMBROIDERY Beads combine very well with embroidery. The two crafts complement each other and a very subtle effect is achieved. Chain stitch filled with seed beads, spider's web with bugle beads, and satin stitch with couched strings of seed beads are just a few exciting combinations.

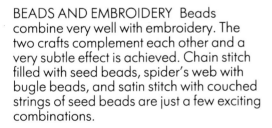

QUILTING

This three-dimensional hand appliqué features lattice quilting in running stitch with French knot flowers on the intersections.

*Q*uilting is both functional and decorative in that it provides warmth and design. The quilting stitches hold the batting (wadding) in place and keep it from bunching. Stitches either follow the outline of shapes in the design or they create decorative patterns on the background. Quilting can be done by hand with a small running stitch or by machine.

BASIC REQUIREMENTS

The following items are required for successful quilting:

Polyester batting (wadding) in large sheets
Polyester wadding for trapunto or stuffed
  shapes
A quilting hoop or ring to hold the layers
  taut for hand quilting
Quilting thread (No 50) (This is a fairly thick
  thread that has been waxed. If it is not
  available, two strands of embroidery
  thread can be used instead.)
Dressmaker's chalk/pencil, water soluble
  quilting pen or soft lead pencil to transfer
  the quilting design (If you use a pencil,
  press very lightly and make dotted rather
  than solid lines.)
Cardboard for making templates if a motif
  is repeated or for intricate patterns

The quilting possibilities on a plain jacket are infinite. Enjoy the designs on the following pages and design your own quilted pocket, panel or collar.

THE TEXTILE SANDWICH

Before you begin quilting, tack the three layers together: first the lining, wrong side up, then the batting (wadding) and then the appliqué or ground fabric, right side up. Tack from the centre out towards each of the corners. Begin quilting in the centre with tiny running stitches or machine stitching, working outwards to prevent puckering.

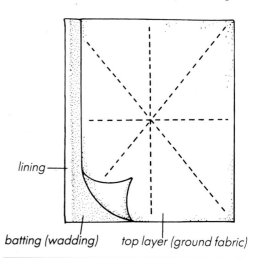

lining

batting (wadding) *top layer (ground fabric)*

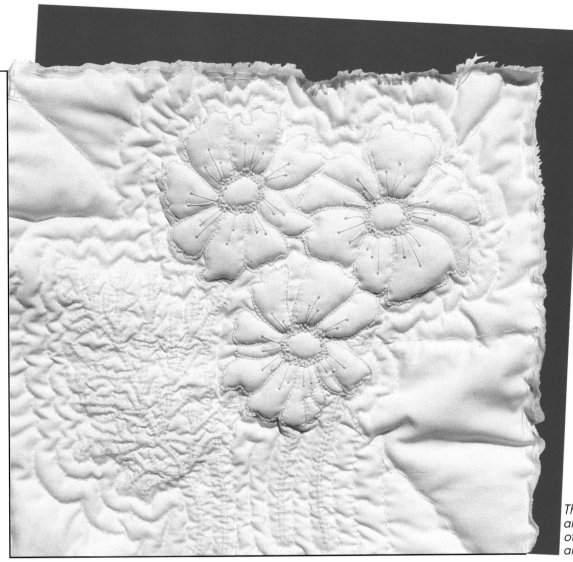

This work is unfinished and the various layers of the 'textile sandwich' are visible.

QUILTING TECHNIQUES

There are a number of different quilting techniques, ranging from high relief (trapunto) to merely the suggestion of quilted rhythms (such as echo quilting).

As there are so many techniques to choose from, it is important to select one that will enhance your design. The following are some of the quilting methods available:

ECHO QUILTING This is a simple method of quilting by echoing the outlines of the basic design. Quilt through all the layers using tiny running stitches (hand quilting). Remember to keep your stitches small and even. Begin at the centre and move outwards at regular intervals or at increasing intervals.

To create echo quilting by machine, position the foot next to the appliqué and straight stitch around the design using the foot space as your guide. Continue quilting until the entire background is patterned.

QUILTING IN PATTERNS Motifs can be made in many different shapes such as flowers, shells or scallops. This type of quilting is done in large negative spaces for added interest or on borders. Motifs can be used singly or for repeat designs. This type of pattern lends itself to trapunto quilting as well.

DIAGONAL OR LATTICE QUILTING Stitch diagonal lines at regular intervals across the top of the design in one direction and then at the same intervals in the opposite direction to form a diamond pattern.

For a subtle effect, French knots can be worked at the intersections of the lattice. Another exciting idea is to make a small embroidered flower, such as a rosebud or forget-me-knot, on the intersecting diagonals.

All the techniques discussed above use the 'textile sandwich' as their base and the finished effect is low relief.

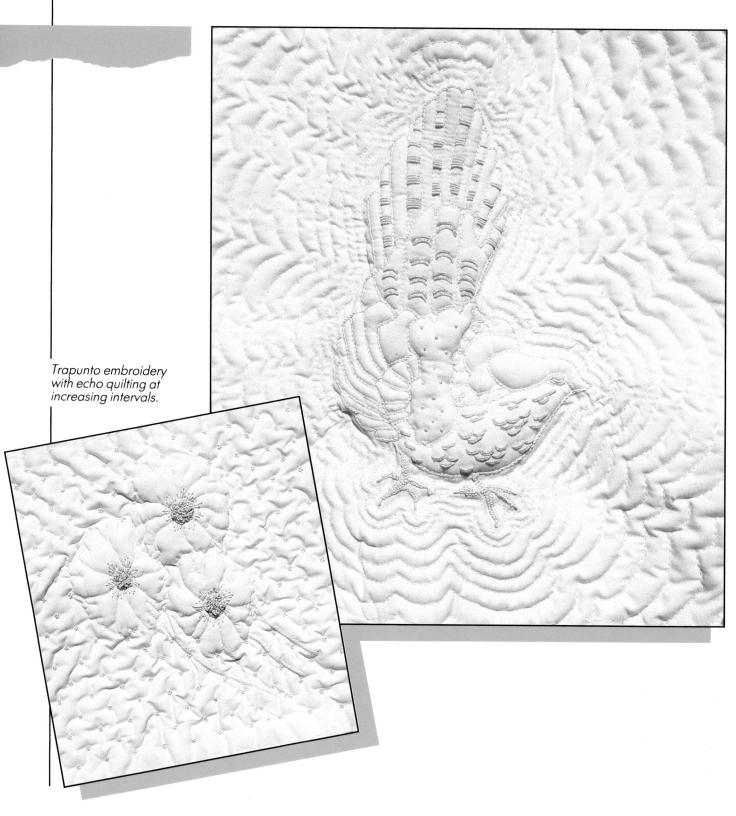

*Trapunto embroidery
with echo quilting at
increasing intervals.*

This little figure was first embroidered; a muslin backing was attached with tiny running stitches around the figure's outline. The muslin was then trapunto quilted for the high-relief effect. Finally a 'textile sandwich' was made for the echo-quilted background.

TRAPUNTO AND CORDED QUILTING

Trapunto and corded quilting are both high relief techniques. The ground fabric and a lining (muslin) are the basic ingredients of this raised type of quilting. After the design has been stuffed (see below), the background can be quilted using the 'textile sandwich' and relevant techniques.

TRAPUNTO or high relief quilting is an attractive form of quilting where selected areas of the design are padded to give a raised effect.

Cut a piece of background fabric and a corresponding piece of muslin. Put them together with the right side of the background fabric on top and transfer the quilting design onto the fabric using a dressmaker's pencil or an erasable marking pen. Secure the fabrics in a quilting hoop and stitch along the design lines in either back stitch or running stitch, making your stitches small and even. Make a small slit in the muslin in the centre of each shape to be padded, or push the weave aside, and insert small pieces of polyester wadding through the slit with the point of a knitting needle or crochet hook until the shape is evenly padded on the right side. Some areas can be padded more than others to create different effects. Sew up the slit with tiny whip stitches.

Trapunto is complemented by background quilting such as Echo Quilting (page 41) or by French knotting (page 31) at regular intervals.

TRAPUNTO AND EMBROIDERY can also be combined successfully. Instead of running stitches, trapunto outlines can be embroidered with chain stitch or French knots (as seen in candlewicking page 44). French knots can be used to delineate the shapes which are then stuffed.

CORDED QUILTING Sometimes called Italian quilting, this type of quilting gives an attractive raised effect which is suitable for linear patterns.

After transferring the design onto the fabric, tack the top fabric and the backing fabric (muslin) together with diagonal, horizontal or vertical lines. Machine straight stitch, or stitch by hand along the parallel lines using back stitch or running stitch.

Working from the back and using a blunt bodkin or tapestry needle threaded with quilting wool or cord, insert the needle between the parallel lines.

To tie off the cord, make a small back stitch into the backing fabric (lining) or if the cord exits close to the beginning, knot the two ends of the cord together. Do not pull the cord too tight — leave a little slack in case of shrinkage when the item is washed.

CANDLEWICKING

In the early American pioneering days, necessity became the mother of invention and beautiful embroidery was created by using the cotton wick from the middle of a candle. Although other embroidery stitches were used, traditional candlewicking was done with pure cotton thread and colonial knots, following the outline of a design. The background fabric was always pure cotton and the work was white on white or cream on cream.

Today candlewicking is made on natural or coloured fabric using the colonial knot or the French knot (one twist for finer detail or two twists for a bolder effect). Four-strand cotton thread is the best yarn to use.

Candlewicking is in fact an embroidery technique which, together with quilting, makes exciting designs and dimensions possible.

BASIC REQUIREMENTS

A pair of scissors
A water-soluble pen
Embroidery needle (Chenille needles are ideal)
An embroidery ring
Beeswax
100% natural or coloured cotton fabric
Candlewicking yarn (crochet cotton or 4 strands of embroidery thread)

1. Place the fabric over the candlewicking pattern. You should be able to see the dots through the fabric. If not, hold the fabric and the pattern up to the light and lightly mark the pattern onto the top side with a marking pen.

2. Insert the fabric into the embroidery ring to hold the fabric taut.

3. Cut the yarn into 50 cm lengths. Run the yarn lightly over the beeswax to hold the threads together.

4. *If you wish to trapunto quilt (page 43) the candlewicking, work with a piece of muslin behind the fabric.* Once the embroidery is complete the muslin can be slit at the back of the design and stuffed with polyester wadding. Close the slit with tiny whip stitches. The background can also be quilted by embroidering French knots through a 'textile sandwich' i.e. top fabric, flat polyester batting (wadding) and lining (see page 40).

5. Work colonial or French knots on the dots (see page 31), and stem stitch or chain stitch along the lines. Work satin stitch or small French knots in the filled-in areas. Other embroidery stitches that I find complementary to candlewicking are whipped chain and woven back stitch. (See pages 26 and 33 for Embroidery Stitches.)

6. Remove the fabric from the ring when all the stitching is complete. Rinse the fabric in cool water to remove the marks left by the marking pen. Now wash again in very hot

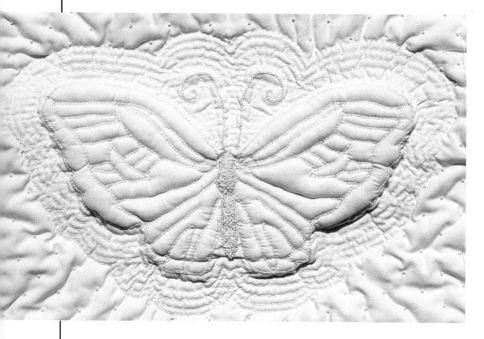

Trapunto quilting and embroidery with a surround of echo quilting.

Fine colonial knots, trapunto quilting and exquisite embroidery.

Note the quilting hoop — an essential piece of candlewicking equipment.

water. This will shrink the fabric, holding the stitches firmly in place. Roll the fabric in a towel to remove the excess water, then allow to dry.

7. Iron the fabric gently on a padded surface with the design face down.

Be adventurous and use coloured embroidery thread when candlewicking and quilting. (See photograph on page 45.) Candlewicking is ideal for pockets, yokes, hems and cuffs. Baby garments, such as christening robes, and evening bags and lingerie cases lend themselves to this technique.

Colonial knots in four-strand cotton thread with trapunto quilting.

2 TAKE THE BASICS

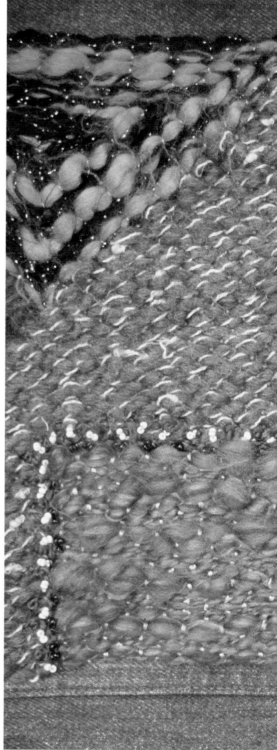

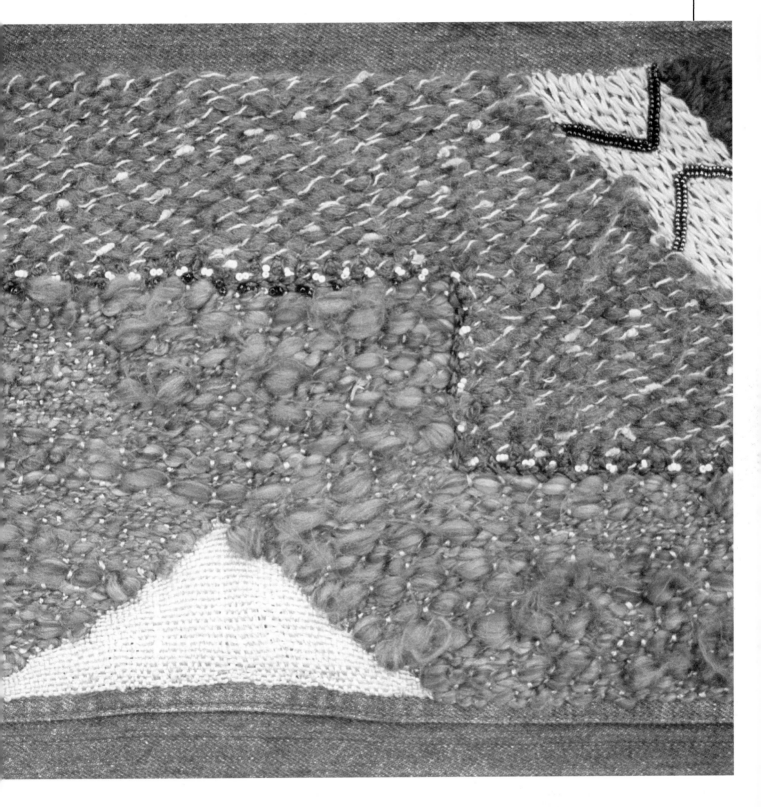

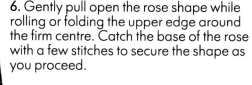

'*Everything is coming up roses.... For that special occasion make a cluster of Dior roses and attach them to your garment or accessory with a few hem stitches. In different colour fabrics the three-dimensional roses will look pleasing appended to a hat, a jersey or belt, or on an elegant evening dress. Organza, satin, taffeta and voile are ideal fabrics.*

Change the colour of the rose by joining two strips of fabric together (one third black and two thirds red). The satin gives an open, full-blown rose shape.

These sketches by young designers from Leggats Academy of Design show the versatility of the basic three-dimensional rose. Large silver roses add a touch of glamour to an evening jersey; a soft leather rose enhances a basic belt.

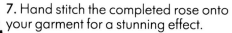

6. Gently pull open the rose shape while rolling or folding the upper edge around the firm centre. Catch the base of the rose with a few stitches to secure the shape as you proceed.

7. Hand stitch the completed rose onto your garment for a stunning effect.

THE DIOR ROSE

1. Cut a 12 x 60 cm rectangle of fabric for each rose. The crosswise grain is ideal but the rose also works on the straight grain.

2. Fold the rectangle lengthways, right sides together, and stitch down the long side and one short end.

3. Trim the seams, turn through and hand stitch the open end, curving the edge slightly.

4. Run a gathering stitch down the long seamed edge, and pull it up, easing slightly at one end and pulling up more firmly at the other.

5. To shape the rose, roll up very tightly from the *lightly* gathered short end towards the well-gathered end.

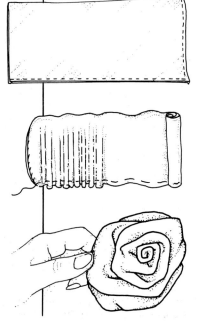

The pastel pink sketch of a beautiful rose was the inspiration for this soft leather belt. The basic belt was made first, with the leather rose added later. (The rose is made by cutting a 40 x 7 cm strip of leather – it does not have to be folded and hemmed as leather does not unravel. Gather, roll and fold, catching the base with small stitches to secure the shape. Cut three leather leaves and attach them to the belt together with the rose.)

Charcoal, platinum and blue roses cascade in a swirl of tulle and silk. A simple idea becomes a glorious hat for that special occasion.

Magenta crepe sets off two taffeta roses on a striking black hat.

Yet another use for the versatile three-dimensional rose as seen in this garland, which is complemented by the 20s-style headband. Notice the subtle change of colour within the rose garland.

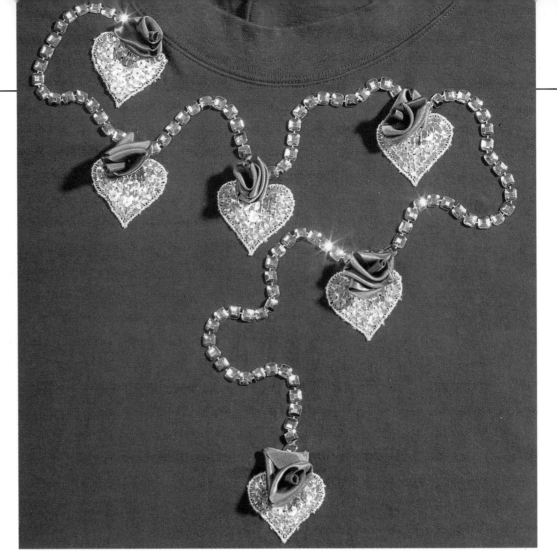

Take an unadorned top and turn it into something really stylish by adding ribbon roses, sequined hearts and bead braid.

HEARTS AND ROSES

Materials for the roses
Approx. 2 metres of satin ribbon 12-38 mm
  wide (width and quantity of ribbon will
  depend on the number and size of
  the roses)
Matching thread
Needle
Scissors

Material for the hearts
A small piece of tulle or organza
Charcoal iron-on vilene
Silver metallic thread
A packet of silver sequins
A bead needle
1 m bead braid to connect the hearts and
  roses

Template (page 166)

1. *For the ribbon roses* form the bud centre of the rose by rolling one end of the ribbon six turns to make a tight tube. Make three small stitches at the base to hold it firm.

2. To form the petals, fold the ribbon as illustrated below so that it is parallel to the tube and forming a 45° angle.

3. Roll the tube across the fold, loosely at the top and tightly at the base. Stitch in place with a couple of stitches.

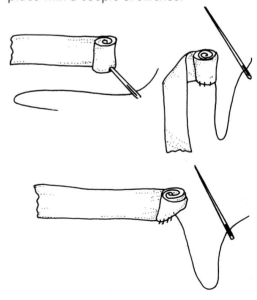

4. Continue to fold, roll and stitch, shaping the rose as you work, until it is the desired size. Finish by turning the raw end under the rose.

5. *For the sequined hearts* trace the hearts directly from the book onto the shiny side of the charcoal vilene.

6. Cut out and iron the hearts onto the tulle or organza. Do not cut out the shapes yet but machine satin stitch the heart outlines in silver metallic thread.

7. Now cut out the overlocked heart shapes and, using a double back stitch (see page 37), attach the sequins.

8. Using the photograph as your guide, hand hem the hearts and roses to the background fabric, then link the design by couching the bead braid in position.

BOWS

Materials
25 cm white silk for the bow
Iron-on vilene
White sewing machine thread
Silver metallic embroidery thread
Tiny pearls and white seed beads
A bead needle

Stitches (pages 26-33)
Laid-work trellis, French knots

Template (page 174)

1. Follow the instructions on page 12 and enlarge the design to suit your garment.

2. Trace, cut and prepare the bow for the Double Vilene Technique (see page 20).

3. Satin stitch the details and all the raw edges with white machine thread. Cut away the excess fabric.

4. Embroider the knot of the bow in laid-work trellis. Crust (page 36) tiny seed beads in the diamond spaces. Stitch the pearls into the loops of the bow and along the crease lines.

5. Work tiny French knots in silver thread on the two long ends.

6. Hand hem the beaded bow onto your garment.

Bows – large or small, black, white or coloured – give instant appeal to a ballet bodice or flimsy gathered skirt.

Add poppies, pansies or scarlet flowers to a basic hat or pair of red leather pumps for that distinctive finishing touch.

SCARLET FLOWERS

Materials
Small pieces of scarlet and emerald chintz
Matching machine thread
Cream and scarlet embroidery thread
Iron-on vilene

Stitches (pages 26-33)
French knots, extended French knots,
 whipped chain stitch

Template (page 142)

1. Trace the flowers and leaves directly onto the shiny side of the vilene. Cut out the shapes and iron them onto the wrong side of the fabric.

2. Cut out the fabric shapes, place them on a larger piece of fabric, wrong sides together, and machine satin stitch the petal divisions and outlines in matching thread. (See page 22 for the Double Fabric Technique.)

3. Using the photograph as your guide, embroider the centre of the flowers in scarlet and cream French knots and extended French knots.

4. Using three strands of embroidery thread, outline the flowers (just inside the satin-stitched outline) in whipped chain stitch.

5. Cut away the excess fabric and assemble the flowers and leaves on the hat or pumps, attaching them with a few invisible hem stitches.

Accent these striking appliqué flowers with embroidery details.

Embellished with beading or embroidery, these bright yellow pansies turn a simple pair of pumps into something quite whimsical.

YELLOW PANSIES

Materials
Small piece of yellow glazed cotton
Iron-on vilene
Matching machine thread
Black, white, red and yellow embroidery
  thread

Stitches (pages 26-33)
Bullion knots, French knots, split stitch, stab
  or straight stitch, running stitch

Template (pages 144-145)

1. Trace, cut and prepare the pansies for the Double Fabric Technique (page 22).

2. Machine satin stitch the petal divisions and outlines in matching thread.

3. Embroider the centres in black bullion knots and yellow French knots.

4. Shade the petals with split stitch, stab stitch and running stitch (see pages 26-33 for Embroidery Techniques).

5. Once all the details have been embroidered, cut away the excess fabric.

6. Using two strands of yellow embroidery thread, hand stitch the pansies to the pumps just inside the satin-stitched outline.

SILK POPPIES

Materials
Small pieces of red silk
Iron-on vilene
Red machine thread
Yellow, green and black embroidery
  thread

Stitches (pages 26-33)
Bullion knots, satin stitch, stem stitch

Template (pages 146-147)

1. Prepare the poppies by following the instructions for the Double Fabric Technique on page 22.

2. Machine satin stitch the poppies in red and cut away the excess fabric.

3. Embroider the centre of each poppy in six yellow bullion knots. Fill in the space with satin stitch, using three strands of green embroidery thread.

4. Stem stitch the stamens in black, adding a yellow bullion knot to each tip.

5. Hand hem the finished poppies to the hat or leather pumps. Leave the upper edge of the poppies free standing if attaching the poppies to the pumps.

Vibrant poppies add a dash of colour to red leather pumps or a black felt hat.

CALABASH BAG

Materials for the basic bag
1 m black or blue denim (or suitable
  bag material)
1 metre of lining
1 zip 45 – 50 cm long
1,20 m piping cord
Matching machine thread

Template (page 173)

1. Using the pattern on page 173, cut out two pieces in denim and two in lining.

2. Cut one strap 12 x 150 cm (for one continuous strap) or cut the strip in two halves (12 x 75 cm) for a knotted strap.

3. Mark the position of the zip on the fabric and machine the small seam at each end of the zip opening. Tack the zip in position and machine stitch in place.

4. Make your piping by covering piping cord with a narrow length of denim, preferably cut on the cross. Tack the piping along the outer edge of one piece of denim. The piping must be facing inwards on the right side of the denim. Machine stitch in position.

5. Attach the appliqué design of your choice (see opposite).

6. *With the zip open* and right sides together, machine stitch along the raw edges of the bag. Trim seams and turn through.

7. Machine stitch the lining, right sides together, as shown in fig 4. Slip the lining into the denim section and hand hem the lining to the zip edge, turning under the seam allowance as you proceed. (Another method of lining the bag is to zigzag the denim and lining together at the start and to treat the pieces as one.)

8. *For the continuous strap,* fold the fabric in half lengthwise, right sides facing, and

machine stitch the raw edges, leaving one end open. Trim and turn through.

9. Slip the raw end of the strap into the opening at the top end of the bag (see fig 3). Turn under a seam allowance on the raw edge of the bag and stitch through all the layers (i.e. bag and strap – 4 layers).

10. Slip the other end of the strap into the opening on the opposite side of the bag and stitch through all the layers.

11. *For the knotted strap,* fold the straps in half lengthwise, right sides facing, and machine stitch the raw edges of each strap, leaving one end open. Turn through. Insert the raw edges into the openings at either side of the bag and stitch through all the layers.

12. Top stitch the strap/straps for a professional finish.

13. Knot the two straps together.

DENIM DAISIES

Materials
Small pieces of suede or leather in shades
  of blue and white
White broderie anglaise fabric
Iron-on vilene
Matching machine thread

Template (page 167)

1. Enlarge the daisies to suit your bag by following the instructions on page 12.

2. Trace, cut and prepare the daisies for the Direct Appliqué Technique on page 18.

3. Satin stitch the broderie anglaise shapes and open zigzag the suede and leather pieces directly onto the right side of the calabash bag fabric (step 5 of Calabash Bag).

4. Now make up the bag as directed opposite.

fig 1

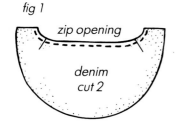

zip opening

*denim
cut 2*

piping facing inwards

fig 2

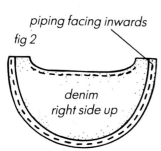

*denim
right side up*

fig 3

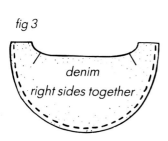

*denim
right sides together*

fig 4

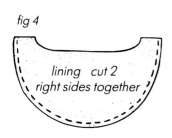

*lining   cut 2
right sides together*

BLUE LEATHER ABSTRACT

Materials
A selection of textured leather in shades
  of blue
A small accent piece of mustard leather
Mustard, beige and blue coton perlé
  embroidery thread
Six washers
A couple of brass studs and eyelets
Blue machine thread

Stitches (pages 26-33)
Chain stitch, buttonhole stitch,
  blanket stitch

1. Cut interesting shapes from your leather
offcuts.

2. Assemble the design directly onto the
background fabric. Be sure to balance the
light and dark shades to make an
interesting composition, and include
twisted strips and plaited lengths.

3. Once you are happy with your design,
machine zigzag or satin stitch the shapes to
the background.

4. Embroider mustard squiggles in chain
stitch through the design.

5. Insert brass studs and eyelets in focal
positions.

6. Cover washers in buttonhole stitch.

7. Cut out a few leather circles and
embroider the edges in blanket stitch.
Attach these circles to the eyelets with a
length of embroidery thread, so they can
dangle.

8. Make up the bag by following the
instructions above.

*This is a bag for all seasons. Make it in blue
or black denim, leather or canvas and add a
complementary design to make it suitable for
day or evening.*

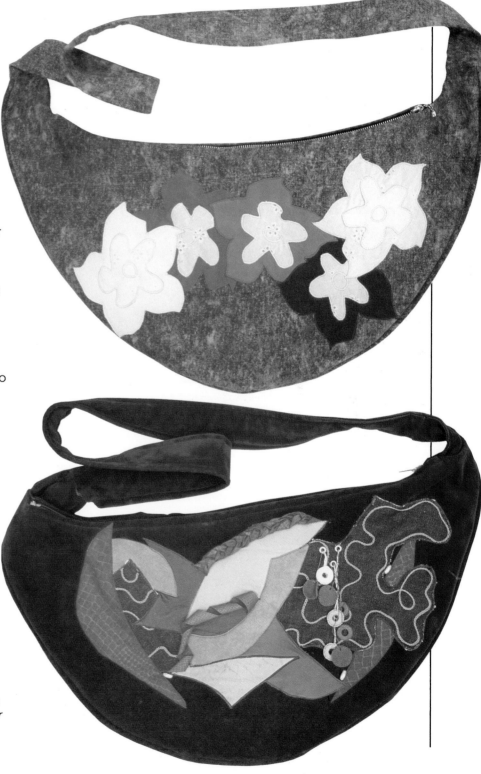

BROWN LEATHER BELT

Materials

Long offcuts of brown leather for the main belt and tiny strap
Offcuts of black leather for the buckle and tongue
Strong machine thread
A leather needle for thick leather or a very sharp needle (i.e. 70) for nappa leather
A leather foot for the machine (a roller or walking foot is particularly good)

Template

Belt with elastic (page 118)
Belt using all leather (pages 118-119)

1. Enlarge the pattern of your choice to fit your waist.

2. If you use wide elastic instead of the brown leather, simply measure your waist so that the elastic fits comfortably around the waist, then add the buckle and tongue to each end.

3. If you use brown leather for the central section, four strips of leather may be joined together or one single piece of leather may be used. If a single piece is used, machine pin tucks along the lines marked on the pattern.

4. Turn under a 5 mm hem along the long edges and top stitch.

5. Cut out the buckle in black leather and top stitch the two layers marked 'A' as shown.

fig 1

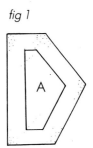

BLACK AND OCHRE

Materials

A selection of textured charcoal, brown and ochre leather
Six brass studs and beads or charcoal and black seed beads
Matching machine thread

Template (page 173)

1. Cut abstract leaf shapes from your leather offcuts. Use the photograph as your guide and assemble the shapes directly onto the background fabric. Glue the leather in position with a glue stick – do not pin as this marks the leather.

2. Machine zigzag or satin stitch in place.

3. Decorate the design with brass studs or seed beads.

4. Now make up the bag by following the instructions on page 54.

6. Cut out pattern 'B' and use a punch to make a hole for the prong. Take the brass centre piece from an old belt and push it through the hole.

fig 2

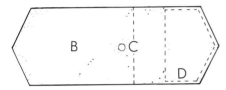

7. Now fold 'B' around 'A' and top stitch along line 'C' as indicated in fig 3.

fig 3

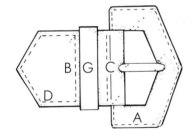

8. Insert one end of the leather belt between the two V-shaped layers of leather ('B') and top stitch along line 'D' as shown in fig 3.

9. For the tongue end, cut two pieces of black leather as per pattern 'E'. Position the brown leather between the V-shaped layers and top stitch around line 'F' as indicated. Use a punch to make the holes.

fig 4

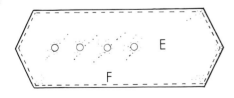

10. Cut out the leather strip for the small strap ('G') in brown leather. Join the ends, then top stitch to give a professional finish. Slip the strap over the tongue end of the belt into position (see fig 3).

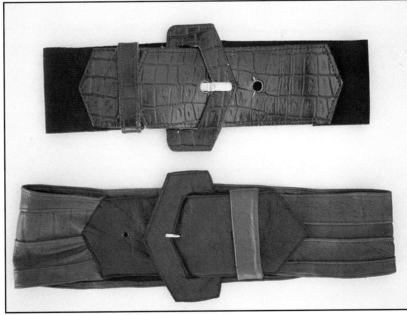

This gorgeous belt was made entirely from scraps of leather. If you do not have enough leather for the centre section, use wide elastic for the main belt with each end made up in leather.

PINK BUTTERFLY

Materials
A piece of pink suede for the wings
A piece of pink velvet for the abdomen
Matching machine thread
A selection of embroidery threads
Four tiny beads for the eyes and the tips
 of the feelers
A looping foot for the abdomen fluff
Iron-on vilene

Stitches (pages 26-33)
Split stitch, bullion knots, spider's webs,
 Roumanian stitch, French knots and
 raised chain stitch

Template (page 117)

1. Trace, cut and prepare the butterfly for
the Double Vilene Technique on page 20.

2. Machine satin stitch the abdomen, wing
divisions and outlines in pink thread.

3. Loop the abdomen (see page 34) using
the looping foot (sometimes called a
tailor's tack foot) and the satin stitch
setting.

4. Using the photograph as a guide and
referring to the embroidery stitches on
pages 26-33, embroider the details: split
stitch decorated with French knots on the
large black and white areas; alternating
black and white bullion knots on the border
of the upper wings; vertical spider's webs
on the outer edge of the wings and
Roumanian stitch bordered with raised
chain stitch on the lower wings.

5. Embroider French knots on the
abdomen. Using black/gold metallic
thread, embroider the feelers in chain stitch
and end with tiny pearl beads. Attach two
tiny bronze beads for the eyes.

BLACK BUTTERFLY

Materials
A piece of black velvet for the main part
 of the butterfly
Small pieces of white moiré taffeta for
 details
White tulle for overlay on the velvet
Scraps of beige high-pile velvet for the
 abdomen
Black or navy, beige and silver machine
 thread
Silver and black/gold metallic embroidery
 thread
White and rust embroidery thread
Two black sequins
Two tiny crystal seed beads for the eyes
Iron-on vilene

Stitches (pages 26-33)
Spider's webs, bullion knots, French knots
 and chain stitch

Template (page 116)

1. Trace, cut and prepare the butterfly for
the Double Vilene Technique (page 20)
using the black velvet.

2. Place a piece of white tulle over the
black velvet shape, then place the white
moiré taffeta in position and the high-pile
velvet on the abdomen. Tack the design
together onto the second piece of vilene.

3. Machine satin stitch all the wing divisions
in navy or black, the abdomen in beige
and the wing outlines in silver.

4. Embroider the details using the
photograph as your guide (spider's webs
in rust, bullion knots in white and French
knots in silver).

5. Chain stitch the feelers with black/gold
metallic thread.

6. Bead the eyes with a black sequin
topped with a crystal seed bead.

Use these exotic butterflies to enhance any simple garment. The basic shape is appliquéd on suede and then 'needle painted' to give the finer details.

OCHRE MOTH

Materials
One small piece of mustard (ochre) velvet
Scraps of cream suede
High-pile velvet for the abdomen
Matching machine thread
Rust, brown and mustard embroidery
  thread
Black/gold metallic embroidery thread
Looping foot for the loops around the
  abdomen
Iron-on vilene

Stitches (pages 26-33)
Chain stitch, satin stitch and French knots

Template (page 115)

1. Trace, cut and prepare the design for the Double Vilene Technique (page 20) using the mustard-coloured velvet.

2. Position the high-pile velvet on the abdomen and the cream suede on the wings as shown. Tack the design together onto a second piece of vilene.

3 Machine satin stitch the wing divisions and outlines.

4. Using the looping foot and following the instructions on page 34, make the mustard loops around the abdomen.

5. Hand embroider the details using the photograph as your guide. Cut away the excess vilene.

Take a basic black jersey and add a cluster of bullion and French knot flowers to the collar.

Step 1

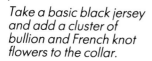

Step 2

Step 3

Step 4

EMBROIDERED FLOWERS

Materials
Donkey-brown and white crochet thread
White, olive and gold-green embroidery
  thread
No. 7 and No. 9 Chenille needles

Stitches (pages 26-33)
Bullion knots, French knots, lazy daisy
stitch, fly stitch

1. Begin the embroidery in the centre of the collar. The *full-blown roses* are a series of looped bullion knots. Using a No. 9 needle, make four 20-twist bullion loops with the point of return as close as possible to the point of entry.

2. Make four bullion loops in the spaces between the first four loops. The loops must look intertwined (see page 32). A pearl bead can be used in the centre of this flower.

3. *For each white daisy*, use a No. 7 needle and crochet thread, or three strands of white embroidery thread, and work 16 bullions each with nine twists. Embroider three French knots in the centres. (See steps 1-4 opposite.)

NOTE The colours are reversed on the back of the collar.

4. For the *French knot clusters*, use a No. 9 needle and three strands of embroidery thread and work two-twist French knots. Start with one knot in the centre and circumvent with five French knots.

5. *For the leaves*, use four strands of embroidery thread and work detached chain stitch (lazy daisy) for the full-blown rose leaves, and detached chain stitch (lazy daisy) with six-twist bullion knot centres for the daisy leaves. Using three strands of embroidery thread, embroider fly stitch leaves for the French knot clusters.

EGYPTIAN FIGURE

Materials

Bronze glazed cotton or satin for the figure
 and throne
Small pieces of fine striped and snakeskin-
 patterned silks
Matching machine thread
Iron-on vilene
A selection of bronze, black and gold seed
 beads
A bead needle

Template (page 150)

1. Enlarge the design to suit your garment
by following the instructions on page 12.

2. Using the Double Vilene Technique on
page 20 prepare the complete design (i.e.
the pharaoh and throne) on the glazed
cotton, then superimpose the silk drapes,
headgear and cushion. Do not forget the
underlap seam allowances where two raw
edges will meet.

3. Tack the entire figure onto the second
piece of iron-on vilene, shiny side away
from the design, and machine satin stitch
all the details and raw edges.

4. Use a fine satin stitch for the pleat details
and the drapes.

5. Couch the collar and bracelets with the
seed beads.

6. Cut away your excess vilene and hand
hem the figure onto the garment.

*Machine appliqué and beadwork transform
this basic black top. Choose glamorous silks
and satins in shades of the Nile to make the
stylized figure.*

BLACK BEADED BUTTERFLY

Materials
25 cm of black chintz for the wings
A small piece of black lace for wing insets
A selection of black sequins, bugle and
  seed beads
Two pearls for the tips of the feelers
A bead needle
Black machine thread
Charcoal and white iron-on vilene

Template (page 151)

1. Follow the instructions on page 12 and enlarge or reduce the design to suit your top.

2. Trace, cut and prepare the butterfly for the Double Vilene Technique (page 20), using the white vilene first. Use the charcoal vilene for the second piece of vilene which protrudes all round the design.

3. Superimpose the black lace insets and satin stitch all the raw edges. Cut away the excess vilene.

4. Tack the overlocked butterfly onto the background fabric and appliqué in position using beadwork (see page 36 for Beading). Bead the outer wings with sequins held in place with three seed beads. Crust the lace sections with seed beads and use a raised combination of sequins and beads for the abdomen (see page 36).

5. For the feelers, sew on alternating seed beads and bugle beads and finish with a pearl.

Black chintz, a touch of lace, beads for dazzle and you have instant success with black on black.

A WINTER'S TALE

Materials
Scraps of black and coral leather
Shells, beads, mother-of-pearl wedges
Exotic black, coral and white wool
Leather foot for the machine
Black machine thread

1. Take a black bouclé top and design a winter's tale. When creating an abstract design, make sure the composition and balance is good. The strong diagonals must be controlled by opposing diagonals or small clusters of interest to stop the movement. Negative shapes are as important as the positive shapes.

2. Begin by 'crinkling' the leather onto the background and satin stitching it in place.

3. Crochet or plait a length of exotic wool and arrange it around the leather appliqué to create balanced negative and positive shapes. Hand hem in place.

4. Integrate the woollen braid and the leather pieces with clusters of odds and ends (shells, buttons, beads).

Odds and ends and a touch of leather make a striking statement.

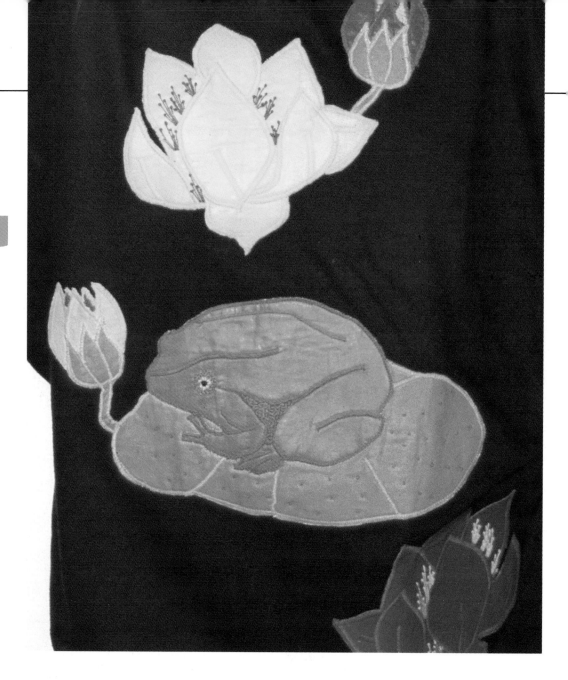

TANGERINE FROG

Materials
25 cm each of tangerine, red, yellow and
 green chintz for the frog, lilies and leaves
Matching machine thread
Black, yellow, tangerine, red and green
 embroidery thread
Iron-on vilene

Stitches (pages 26-33)
Spider's webs, French knots and extended
 French knots

Template (page 164)

1. Enlarge the design by following the
instructions on page 12.

2. Trace, cut out and prepare the frog,
water lilies and leaves for the Double
Vilene Technique on page 20.

3. Machine satin stitch the details and all
the raw edges of the frog, lilies and leaves.
Do not cut away the excess vilene.

4. Using the photograph as a guide,
embroider a spider's web, beginning with
black and changing to yellow, for the
frog's eye; French knot the belly of the frog
and the centre of the lily buds. Embroider
extended French knots in the centres of the
open lilies.

5. Cut away the excess vilene and stitch the
appliqués onto the tank top either by
machine straight stitching just inside the
satin-stitched border or with open zigzags.

BLUE AND BLACK LEATHER FOX

Materials
Black, blue and white leather offcuts
Matching machine thread
Iron-on vilene
Two black beads (rhinestones) for the eyes
A bead needle
A glue stick
A leather foot is recommended

Template (page 154)

1. Following the instructions on page 12, enlarge or reduce the design to suit your garment.

2. Use the Double Vilene Technique (page 20) for the appliqué if the background fabric has stretch, and the Direct Appliqué Technique (page 18) if the background is non-stretch fibre.

3. Machine satin stitch all the details using a leather needle for thick leather or a very sharp needle for fine leather. Work from the centre outwards to prevent puckering.

4. Attach two black beads to the appliqué for the eyes.

5. If using the Double Vilene Technique, hand hem or machine straight stitch the fox to the garment.

Make this striking abstraction of a fox and add it to a winter ensemble.

The dazzle of the beads in the Aztec Sun gives an illusion of radiating rays of light. The combination of silver, gold and bronze sequins serves to reinforce the visual impact.

AZTEC SUN

Materials
A selection of silver, gold and bronze
  sequins, seed beads and bugle beads
1 ball of gold metallic embroidery thread
A small piece of red cotton fabric for
  the face
Polyester wadding for the face
Iron-on vilene
Bead needle
Matching machine thread

Stitches (pages 26-33)
Chain stitch

Template (page 163)

1. Enlarge the design by following the
instructions on page 12.

2. Trace the sun's rays onto the iron-on
vilene, shiny side down.

3. Cut out the shapes and iron them in
position onto your garment.

4. Sketch or trace the centre circle and
facial details directly onto the fabric.

5. Bead the sun's face referring to page 36
for the choice of bead technique.

6. Attach the sequins to the garment with
the corresponding colour seed beads. Use
a double thread and begin with a knot and
a back stitch when beading.

7. Embroider the outer circle of the face in
chain stitch with gold metallic thread.

8. Cut a circle of red fabric 1 cm larger than
the sun's face. Turn the 1 cm seam
allowance under and hand hem this circle
to the back of the design, filling the cavity
with polyester wadding as you close the
shape.

UNISEX NAVY AND
RED JACKET

Materials
Long strips of interesting navy and red
 fabrics
Lace and rickrack offcuts
Buckles
A small scrap of red chintz
Iron-on vilene
Green embroidery thread for the apple
Red machine thread

Template
Apple (page 171)

1. Cut out your jacket pattern.

2. Design interesting vertical shapes from
your navy and red fabrics and assemble
the cut-outs onto the background fabric
using the photograph as your guide.

3. Tack all the shapes, rickrack and lace in
position, then machine satin stitch all the
raw edges with red machine thread.

4. Trace, cut and prepare the red apple for
the Direct Appliqué Technique (page 18)
and machine satin stitch it directly onto the
back panel.

5. Embroider the leaf in satin stitch with
three strands of green embroidery thread.

6. Hand stitch buckles (or zips and buttons)
onto the focal strips for a humorous note.

*Gather together a
selection of interesting
textures in red and navy:
sprigs, seersucker, velvet,
leather and quilted
denim and add lace,
rickrack, buckles and an
appliquéd apple to a
basic denim jacket.*

PATSY'S NDEBELE JACKET

Materials
A selection of brightly coloured chintz
   approx. 25 cm wide
Black machine thread
Iron-on vilene
Large and small multi-coloured African
   beads
A bead needle

Template (page 170)

1. Using a jacket pattern of your own
choice, cut out the jacket front and pocket.

2. Enlarge the geometric templates to the
required size by following the instructions
on page 12.

3. Trace, cut and prepare the shapes for
the Direct Appliqué Technique (page 18).

4. Tack the entire design onto the jacket
front and the pocket and machine satin
stitch all the raw edges in black, working
from the centre outwards to avoid
puckering.

5. Thread long strings of multi-coloured
beads and couch them in position on the
geometric shapes (see page 36 for
Beading Techniques).

6. Make up the jacket as per the
instructions accompanying the pattern.

*Multi-coloured chintz and beads combine
well on denim to create an earthy, African-
inspired garment.*

Left The multi-coloured chintz shapes make this jacket an excellent co-ordinate. The abstract design is appliqué and decorated with exciting beadwork.

Interesting geometric shapes, built up into a glorious pyramid, accent the line of a stylish black denim jacket.

DESIGNS ON DENIM

Material
Small pieces of multi-coloured chintz
Matching machine thread
Iron-on vilene
A selection of multi-coloured beads i.e. seed beads, bugle beads and sequins
A bead needle

Template (page 152)

1. Follow the instructions on page 12 and enlarge or reduce the design to suit your jacket.

2. Using the Double Vilene Technique on page 20, prepare and satin stitch each shape in self colour.

3. Use the photograph as your placement guide and iron the overlocked shapes onto the jacket. (If the vilene does not stick firmly to the garment, tack the shapes in position.) Secure the appliqué to the garment with clever beading combinations (see page 36 for beading techniques).

GEOMETRIC PYRAMID

Materials
25 cm each of turquoise, purple, shocking pink, yellow, navy and white chintz
Iron-on vilene
Black machine thread

Template (page 172)

1. Enlarge the design by following the instructions on page 12.

2. Trace, cut and prepare the shapes for the Direct Appliqué Technique (page 18). Remember to add underlap seam allowances where two raw edges meet.

3. Tack the entire design onto the background fabric and machine satin stitch in black. Work from the centre outwards to avoid puckering.

NOTE If the jacket is already made up, you may prefer to make the pyramid design using the Double Vilene Technique on page 20 and attaching it to the back panel by hand hemming or machine straight stitching just inside the satin-stitched outline.

FLOWER POWER

COSMOS QUILTED BAG

Materials for the flowers
Small pieces of glazed cotton (shades of pink to magenta and white)
Matching machine thread
Yellow embroidery thread
Iron-on vilene

Stitches (pages 26-33)
French knots, extended French knots

Template (page 168)

1. Make the cosmos using the Double Fabric Technique on page 22.

2. Machine satin stitch all the petal divisions and the raw edges.

3. Crust the centres of each daisy in French knots and extended French knots.

4. Cut away the excess fabric if you have not already done so. (In order to protect the outer edge of the design, I often leave all the excess fabric trimming until after the hand work has been completed.)

5. Hand hem the completed cosmos onto the bag. If you want a three-dimensional effect, leave some of the petals free standing (see page 23).

Materials for the bag
72 x 42 cm piece moiré taffeta for basic bag
72 x 42 cm piece glazed cotton for the lining
Three 24 x 42 cm pieces of glazed cotton for 3 inside pockets
1 card of white satin piped bias binding
3 strips of 42 cm long braid for pocket edges
25 cm narrow white ribbon for buttonhole loops
4 pearl buttons
White machine thread
72 x 42 cm piece polyester batting (wadding)

1. Place the polyester batting (wadding) between the moiré taffeta and glazed cotton and tack the layers together.

2. Mark vertical lines 3 cm apart to use as your quilting guide (or follow the water marks of the moiré taffeta).

3. Machine stitch (quilt) the layers together, stopping 1 cm short of the edges. (If you have a machine which does fancy stitches, set the machine on serpentine.)

4. Using the zipper foot, stitch the piped bias binding to the outer edge of the quilted fabric (see NOTE).

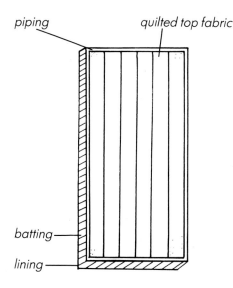

piping   quilted top fabric

batting

lining

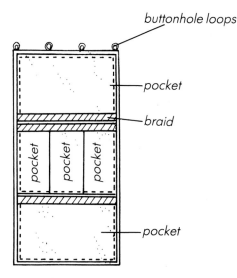

buttonhole loops

pocket

braid

pocket   pocket   pocket

pocket

5. Turn one long edge under on each of the three pocket pieces and trim with a narrow braid.

6. Tack and top stitch the pocket panels to the quilted fabric, turning the raw edges under so that the piping just protrudes.

7. Machine stitch the middle pocket through all the layers to form three smaller pockets.

8. Attach the four buttons on the moire side of the bag, one third down on the machine stitched line of the pocket. Make looped buttonholes with the narrow white ribbon.

9. Fold the bag in thirds. Use it as a clutch bag or add a silk corded strap to make a slingbag.

Add a cascade of wild daisies (cosmos) to a quilted bag. Choose shades of pink and white glazed cotton and finish with deep yellow embroidered French knots.

NOTE If you find piped bias binding difficult to use, the bag can be finished off with plain bias binding once all the pockets are complete.

QUILTED ROSE

Materials
Quantities will depend on the garment

Natural fibres (such as raw silk, cotton, linen or wool) are ideal for this design
Muslin for the trapunto backing
Lining for background quilting
Polyester batting (wadding) for background quilting
Soft bundles of polyester wadding for trapunto quilting
Crochet cotton

Stitches (pages 26-33)
Stem stitch, chain stitch, back stitch and French knots

Template (page 169)

1. Enlarge the design to suit your pattern by following the instructions on page 12.

2. Draw the design onto the right side of your fabric with an erasable marking pen or use dressmaker's carbon.

3. Cut a piece of muslin the same size as your pattern. Tack the muslin behind the top fabric. (See Quilting on page 40.)

4. Embroider all the outlines in chain stitch using a fine crochet cotton.

5. Following the instructions on page 43, trapunto quilt the main petals.

6. Embroider the internal petals in back stitch. Make sure that you pull the threads firmly through all the layers to achieve the quilted effect.

7. Embroider (*do not quilt*) French knots in the centres of the small roses, and stem stitch the veins on the leaves.

8. For the background quilting, make a textile sandwich (page 40) and echo quilt the background in tiny running stitches. Increase the intervals as you move outwards.

ROSETTE

Materials
Quantities will depend on the size of the pattern piece to be candlewicked.

100% pure cotton or good natural fibre such as raw silk or linen for your background
Muslin for trapunto quilting
Soft bundle of polyester wadding for the trapunto
Polyester batting (wadding) for the background quilting
Lining
Crochet thread or coton perlé embroidery thread
4-strand pure cotton thread

Stitches (pages 26-33)
Stem stitch, colonial knots, running stitch and French knots

Template (page 120)

1. Transfer the design onto the background fabric (see page 44 for instructions).

2. Tack the muslin layer behind the top fabric and stem stitch the rosette outlines using a fine crochet cotton, and the photograph as your guide.

3. Now do the candlewicking just inside the stem stitch outlines, using 4-strand pure cotton thread and a colonial knot (see page 31 for Stitches). (Little hearts can be embroidered in the corners if desired.)

4. Make a tiny slit in the muslin behind each 'feather' shape and lightly stuff with soft polyester wadding. (If you include corner hearts, stuff these as well.)

5. Prepare a textile sandwich (page 40) and with a fine crochet cotton or quilting thread, make tiny running stitches through all the layers, working from the centre outwards.

6. Finish the centre of the rosette with a cluster of French knots.

Cream on cream has always been a favourite of mine. Design a garment around this quilted rose and enjoy the exciting dimensions in trapunto and echo quilting.

This design combines candlewicking, trapunto quilting and a lattice background. Reduce or enlarge the pattern to make borders, panels and pockets.

Play with a combination of embroidery stitches and design a Victorian Posy for a pocket, yoke or bag.

VICTORIAN POSY

Materials
50 cm of cream cotton for background or
  cut double fabric from your pocket or
  yoke pattern
Cream machine thread
A selection of embroidery threads for
  the posy

For a quilted background
A piece of polyester batting (wadding) and
  a piece of muslin, the same size as your
  embroidered pattern piece
Ecru quilting thread
Ecru lace for trimming (optional)

Stitches (pages 26-33)
Lazy daisy stitch, French knots, spider's
  webs, bullion knots, Pekinese stitch,
  extended French knots, back stitch,
  Roumanian stitch

Template (page 148)

1. Cut your background material to the size required. Pin the drawing of the posy behind the fabric. Hold the fabric up to the light (against a windowpane) and lightly draw the posy onto the fabric.

2. Using three strands of embroidery thread for the flowers and two for the leaves and stems, follow the stitch guide on page 148. Refer to the embroidery instructions on pages 26-33. If desired, small posies can be repeated in the four corners of the pocket.

3. *For a quilted background*, cut a piece of muslin and polyester batting (wadding) the same size as the pocket or yoke and tack it behind the embroidered panel.

4. Work tiny running stitches around the embroidered posy using two strands of embroidery or quilting thread. (See page 41 for Echo quilting.)

5. Finish off the pocket or yoke with lace, piping or bias binding if desired.

FLOWER POTS

Materials
Small scraps of floral fabric
Tiny pieces of terracotta cotton for the
  flower pots
Shades of pink, burgundy and green
  embroidery thread
Matching machine thread
Iron-on vilene

Stitches (pages 26-33)
Pekinese stitch, bullion roses, lazy daisy
  stitch, Roumanian stitch

Template (page 149)

1. Enlarge or reduce the design to suit your garment by following the instructions on page 12.

2. Trace, cut and prepare the flower pot for the Double Vilene Technique on page 20.

3. Iron a piece of vilene onto the back of a piece of floral fabric for the flowers. Cut out the design in an interesting shape, following the flowers in the fabric design.

4. Tack the flowers and flower pot onto a second sheet of vilene and satin stitch all the raw edges in matching machine thread. Cut away the excess vilene.

5. Hand embroider Pekinese flowers, bullion roses and lazy daisies onto the floral fabric, using three strands of embroidery floss or coton perlé embroidery thread. Embroider Roumanian stitch for the leaves.

6. Hand hem the flower pots onto your garment.

Take a small piece of floral design fabric and add a flower pot and embroidery details for an instant appliqué on a calico yoke.

BIRDS OF A FEATHER

WOOLLEN TOUCAN

Materials
A selection of smooth and chunky wools
  Bronze, gold and silver crochet thread
Embroidery thread or matching machine
  thread for couching some of the chunky
  wools
Iron-on vilene
A selection of needles (fine and
  wool/tapestry needles)

Stitches (pages 26-33)
Chain stitch, split stitch, raised chain stitch,
  buttonhole stitch, Roumanian stitch,
  bullion knots and spider's webs.

Template (pages 138-139)

1. Trace the bird directly from the book
onto your vilene, shiny side downwards.

2. Cut out the shape and iron it onto the
right side of the garment. Using the
photograph as your guide, couch the
chunky wools in place and embroider
chain stitch, split stitch, raised chain stitch,
buttonhole and Roumanian stitch for the
finer wool areas.

3. Couch or knit the wings. Use garter stitch
on fairly coarse needles and cast on and
off to make interesting wings.

4. Embroider the claws using metallic
thread and bullion knots.

5. Work a two-tone spider's web for the
eyes: begin with spokes of one colour and
weave around the centre once or twice
and then change to the other colour.

6. Couch the branch in wool that tones with
the background of the garment. For a
particularly interesting effect make knots in
the wool every now and again to give a
really 'gnarled' effect.

*Take a chunky knit pullover or a jacket and
embroider a gaily-coloured toucan onto the
back of it. This woollen bird is made up of
traditional stitches in modern wools.*

WOOLLEN PARROT

Materials

A selection of tapestry needles suitable for
  wool work
Iron-on vilene
Pencil
Scissors
Black and white embroidery thread
A selection of interesting wools (fine,
  chunky and variegated)

Stitches (pages 26-33)
Couching, Roumanian stitch, chain stitch,
  whipped chain stitch, raised chain stitch,
  spider's web, Pekinese stitch and bullion
  knots

Template (page 155)

1. Enlarge or reduce the design to suit your
garment by following the instructions on
page 12.

2. Place the iron-on vilene, *shiny side
down*, over the drawing and trace the
design onto the vilene, using a soft pencil.
Cut out the pieces on the pencilled
outlines.

3. Position the vilene design, shiny side
down, on the background fabric or
garment and iron in position.

Study the glossary of embroidery stitches
on pages 26-33 and choose stitches that
are suitable for your particular wool.
Couching is ideal for wools that are too
thick to pull through the fabric. The woven
stitches – raised chain, whipped chain and
woven back stitch – are also suitable for
the chunky wools where the base stitch is
made using a fine wool or crochet cotton
and the top work is done in the heavy
wool.

4. If desired, copy this particular design of
the parrot by embroidering as follows: the
beak in chain stitch; the eye in spider's web
or bullion knots using white and black
embroidery thread ; the crown in couching;
the shoulders in Pekinese stitch; the upper

wings in couching or garter stitch (see Note
below); the wing tips in Roumanian stitch;
the claws in bullion knots, and the tail in
whipped chain. The small birds follow the
same basic stitches while the branch is
embroidered in raised chain stitch.

*NOTE If you can knit, the option of garter
stitch instead of couching can be great
fun. Cast on and off to get interesting
shapes.*

*This design is a
wonderful extension of
traditional embroidery
using those leftover balls
of wool. It looks stunning
on a knitted pullover or
jacket. Have fun with the
design and use different
wools and colour
combinations.*

This little penguin was designed by a 12-year-old art student. The pencil crayon sketch was the preliminary drawing for the penguin appliqué.

NOTE A handy hint when working with black is to use charcoal-coloured vilene for the second piece of vilene. White vilene would be noticeable against the black fabric should you fail to trim the excess vilene close to the satin stitching.

PENGUIN

Materials
Small pieces of black, white, orange and yellow satin
Black and yellow machine thread
Black, white and green seed beads
Red and white sequins
A bead needle
Iron-on vilene

Template (page 130)

1. Trace the penguin directly from the back of the book. Follow the instructions for the Double Vilene Technique on page 20 and make up the penguin.

2. Bead the eye with a white seed bead surrounded by a ring of black seed beads. (See Couching Beads on page 36).

3. Sequin the bow tie with small white sequins superimposed on large red sequins, and held in place with green seed beads (see Sequins on page 37).

4. Cut away the excess vilene and hand hem or machine stitch the penguin onto the background fabric.

EARLY BIRDS

Materials
Small pieces of white and terracotta glazed cotton
Terracotta machine thread
Black, white, mustard, terracotta and turquoise embroidery thread
Iron-on vilene

Stitches (pages 26-33)
Roumanian stitch, raised chain stitch, stab stitch, buttonhole bars, French knots, spider's webs, satin stitch

Template (page 141)

1. Trace, cut and prepare the two birds for the Double Vilene Technique (page 20), making one bird white with superimposed terracotta wings, and one terracotta with superimposed white wings.

2. Machine satin stitch all the raw edges in terracotta thread.

3. Use the photograph as your guide and embroider the details using two strands of embroidery thread: legs and tails in Roumanian stitch; the wings in raised chain and stab stitch; the necks in buttonhole bars; the bodies in stab stitch; the heads in French knots; the eyes in spider's webs and the beaks in satin stitch.

4. Trim away the excess vilene and hand hem the completed birds to the yoke.

These early birds are simple appliqués given accent and interest with the addition of embroidery. The turquoise thread and terracotta glazed cotton are a pleasant combination with calico.

OWL AND TWO ROBIN REDBREASTS

Materials
Small scraps of apricot velvet and white cotton for the owl
Small scraps of beige, red, green and white cotton for the robins
Black, blue, brown, yellow and beige embroidery thread
A small ball of yellow wool
Iron-on vilene

Stitches (pages 26-33)
Bullion knots, satin stitch, back stitch

Templates (page 140)

1. Trace the designs directly from the book onto your iron-on vilene and make the tiny birds by following the instructions for the Double Vilene Technique on page 20.

2. Once all the fabrics have been overlocked, embroider the eyes and beaks in satin stitch and back stitch.

3. Embroider bullion knots for the eyebrows.

4. For the woollen brim on the bonnets, wrap the yellow wool around a pencil. Slip the loops off the shaft and secure them by machine stitching down the middle (see page 34). Place the loops on the appliqué design and machine top stitch in place. Cut the ends of the loops to give a furry brim. (Loops can also be made by using a wire hanger – see page 34.)

5. Hand hem the little birds in position on the seam line of jeans or peeping out of a pocket.

These dear little birds lend an enchanting feel to toddlers' jeans.

From a design of Eastern origin, this exotic bird is a beautiful example of hand appliqué. The shapes are stuffed for added dimension and the embroidery is both decorative and functional.

EXOTIC BIRD

Materials
Interesting textures in shades of grey (silk, satin, moiré taffeta and wool)
A small piece of rust velvet and peach cotton for the comb and beak
Embroidery thread in shades of grey and coral
Mustard and black embroidery floss for the eye
Iron-on vilene
Soft bundles of wadding for raised areas

Stitches (pages 26-33)
Whipped chain stitch, stab stitch, Pekinese stitch, French knots, extended French knots, buttonhole bars, bullion knots, spider's webs and Roumanian stitch

Template (page 114)

1. Enlarge or reduce the design to suit your garment by following the instructions on page 12. Trace, cut and prepare the pieces for the Hand Appliqué Technique (page 14).

2. Tack the shapes in position, turning under the seam allowance.

3. Using the photograph as your guide, embroider the shapes in place. Handle the outlines first, inserting a little polyester wadding into the cavities as you close each shape. Use whipped chain, stab stitch, Pekinese and blind hemming to attach the shapes (see pages 26-33 on Embroidery).

4. Add embroidery details to suggest feathers, such as extended French knots, buttonhole bars, bullion knots and French knots, pulling firmly through the wadding to give a quilted effect.

5. Embroider the legs in vertical spider's webs and the claws in Roumanian stitch. For a really exciting effect, vary the number of strands and the ratio (e.g. two grey and one coral or one grey and two coral).

6. Embroider the eye in black and coral bullion knots and the outline in a mustard buttonhole bar.

FLYING GOOSE

Materials
25 cm of rust or terracotta glazed cotton
Small pieces of black and blue glazed
  cotton
Brown, beige and green suede
Matching machine thread
Iron-on vilene
A selection of rust, black and blue beads
A bead needle

Template (page 162)

1. Following the instructions on page 12, enlarge or reduce the design to suit your garment.

2. Make up the goose using the Double Vilene Technique on page 20: trace the entire goose onto the iron-on vilene, cut out and iron the vilene shape onto the rust fabric.

3. Prepare the other shapes and superimpose the other colours, remembering to add the underlap seam allowances where two raw edges will meet.

4. Glue the design in position on the second piece of vilene, using a stick of glue to avoid pin marks on the suede. Machine satin stitch the details and raw edges.

5. Decorate the goose with bead details using the photograph as your guide (see page 36 for beading techniques).

6. Cut away the excess vilene and hand hem or machine straight stitch the flying goose onto your garment.

Suede and glazed cotton complement each other in this flying goose design.

CANDY STICK CLOWN

Materials
25 cm of each primary colour for the shirt
  and pants
25 cm sprigged fabric for neck tie of
  No. 2 clown
A selection of white, red, yellow, blue and
  green cotton fabrics for small details
25 cm ribbon in each primary colour
One large red button
One card each red and white rickrack
Red, black and blue embroidery thread
1 metre yellow soutache (cord) for the
  shoelaces of No. 1 clown
Matching machine thread
Iron-on vilene

Template (page 156)

1. Enlarge or reduce the design to suit your
garment by following the instructions on
page 12.

2. If the background fabric is non-stretch,
use the Direct Appliqué Technique on
page 18, but if the background fabric
stretches use the Double Vilene Technique
on page 20 and prepare all the shapes.

3. Satin stitch the details and all the raw
edges on the clown and umbrella.

4. Hand embroider the face using the
photograph as your guide.

5. *For clown No. 1*, tuck a real hankie into
the pocket.

6. For the shoelaces, work bullion bars and
thread the soutache through these loops.

7. For the candy stick, intertwine the red
and white rickrack, holding each
intersection in place with alternating red
and white French knots.

8. Assemble the clown onto the
background, tuck the ribbons under the
face and machine straight stitch the design
onto the background fabric just inside the
satin-stitched outline.

9. Stitch a large red button onto the braces.

10. *For clown No. 2* make a real bow for
his neck tie using the sprigged fabric.
Take a long rectangle and fold it in half
lengthwise. With right sides together,
machine along the raw long edge. Turn
through to the right side. Cut the two short
sides into V-shapes, tuck the ends under
and top stitch. Tie into a bow.

11. For the diagonal brace, follow the
instructions for the neck tie. Sew on a large
red button.

12. Using the photograph as your guide,
embroider the child's birth details onto the
pocket; trim the shoes with rickrack and
ribbon; and see No. 7 above for
instructions on how to make the candy
stick. Machine straight stitch the finished
clown to the background fabric.

*These happy fellows
show the versatility of
appliqué and two
different interpretations
from the same design.*

The tree trunk is home to these little animal folk.

Create stylish and original garments by adding one of these delightful appliqué designs to a child's basic T-shirt or tracksuit.

TREE FOLK

Materials
25 cm brown linen for tree trunk
Small pieces of red, white, cream, green, pink and beige cotton for tree folk
An assortment of embroidery threads for facial details and leaves on tree
Small ball of yellow knitting yarn for birds' bonnets
Iron-on vilene

Stitches (pages 26-33)
Satin stitch, back stitch, stab stitch, Roumanian stitch

Template (page 126)

1. Enlarge the design if necessary by following the instructions on page 12.

2. Make all the creatures and the tree separately, using the Double Vilene Technique (page 20).

3. Once all the shapes have been machine satin stitched, embroider the eyes and beaks of the birds in satin stitch and back stitch.

4. Use stab stitch for the hedgehog's quills and Roumanian stitch for the leaves.

5. For the woollen brim of the bonnets, wrap the yellow wool around a pencil, slip the loops off the shaft and secure them by machine stitching down the middle (see page 34). Place the loops on the appliqué and machine top stitch them in place. Cut the ends of the loops to give a furry brim.

6. Attach the tree and the tree folk to the T-shirt by hand hemming them in place or by machine straight stitching inside the satin-stitched outline.

TOADSTOOL HOUSES

Materials

25 cm each red, apricot, navy, green, turquoise and grey glazed cotton for toadstools
Small pieces of grey cotton for the mice
Small piece of cotton with tiny spots for the apron
Small pieces of pink cotton for the ears
Small pieces of fun fluff fabric for the snow
Small scraps for the chimney pots
Black and white embroidery thread
Piece of polyester wadding
Iron-on vilene

Stitches (pages 26-33)
Satin stitch, chain stitch and French knots

Templates (pages 158-159)

1. Enlarge the design if necessary by following the instructions on page 12.

2. Follow the Double Vilene Technique on page 20 and make the toadstool houses and mice. Trim away the excess vilene and embroider the little faces with satin stitch noses and eyes.

3. Highlight the eyes with a white French knot and work a black French knot for the eyebrows. Chain stitch the mouths.

4. Cut a piece of wadding the shape of the toadstools and assemble the appliqué on the garment over the wadding. Machine straight stitch them in place just inside the satin-stitched outlines.

BALLET PUMPS

Materials
Small pieces of cream satin and cotton for the pumps
1 card of satin piped bias binding
1 m x 1 cm wide cream satin ribbon
Matching machine thread
Iron-on vilene

Template (page 160)

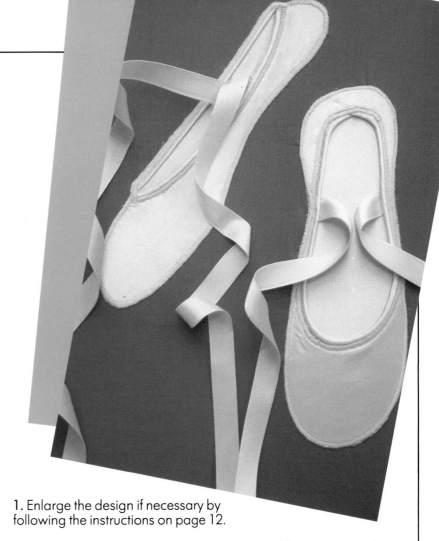

1. Enlarge the design if necessary by following the instructions on page 12.

2. Trace the complete ballet pump onto the shiny side of the iron-on vilene.

3. Cut out the shapes and iron them onto the wrong side of the fabrics.

4. Cut out the vilene-backed shapes and position the satin upper shape on the cream cotton base, inserting the piped bias binding between the two layers.

5. Tack the bias binding close to the outer edge and place the prepared pumps onto the non-shiny side of a larger piece of vilene.

6. Machine satin stitch the pumps, using a zipper foot around the piped edge.

7. Cut away the excess vilene and iron the ballet pumps directly onto the garment. Hand hem or machine stitch in place.

8. Cut the ribbon into four lengths and hand hem them onto the shoes, referring to the photograph for placement. Loop the loose ends and secure them with a couple of tiny invisible stitches.

These pumps make an ideal appliqué for any young ballet enthusiast.

A bundle of fluffy mischief at the end of a ski-jump makes a delightful winter motif for a bright red pullover or tracksuit top.

SKI-JUMP TUMBLE

Materials
Small pieces of spotted, sprigged and
  striped cotton fabric for scarves and hat
Small scraps of apricot velvet for two
  bodies; beige linen for three bodies
Cream and pink fun fluff (synthetic
  material) for the muzzles, chests, hat trim
  and ear muffs
Apricot cotton for skis
White cotton for eyes
Matching machine thread
Blue, white, black and light brown
  embroidery thread
Iron-on vilene

Stitches (pages 26-33)
Satin stitch, French knots, bullion knots,
  chain stitch and buttonhole bars

Template (page 137)

1. Prepare each little creature for the
Double Vilene Technique (see page 20).

2. Once all the raw edges have been
overlocked, hand embroider the details on
the faces: satin stitch the eyes, bullion knot
the eyebrows and work buttonhole bars for
the mouths (see pages 26-33 for
Embroidery Techniques).

3. Assemble the creatures to suit your
pullover, using the photograph as your
guide.

4. Tack in position and hand hem with
matching machine thread.

LITTLE BONNETS

Materials
Tiny pieces of liberty cotton
Broderie anglaise fabric
Broderie anglaise lace and narrow ribbon
1 m of silk cord for the hair
A selection of embroidery threads to suit your dress fabric
A small piece of raw silk for the two baskets
Iron-on vilene
Polyester batting (wadding) and lining for quilting

Stitches (pages 26-33)
Roumanian stitch, buttonhole bars, running stitch, chain stitch, French knots, extended French knots, bullion rosebuds

Templates (pages 128-129)

1. Cut out your yoke or pocket. Enlarge or reduce your design to fit the pattern piece by following the instructions on page 12.

2. Trace, cut and prepare the appliqué piece for the Direct Appliqué Technique (page 18). Machine satin stitch all the details and raw edges.

3. Draw the shoes and socks onto the appliquéd fabric and embroider the socks in Roumanian stitch and the shoes in buttonhole or chain stitch.

4. Embroider extended French knots for the grass. Using the photograph as your guide, work bullion rosebuds, French knots and chain stitch for the flowers. Embroider the leaves in Roumanian stitch.

5. Following the instructions on page 34, make the hair by pulling the silk coils from the cord and attaching them to the bonnets under the lace brim or behind the bows.

6. Finish off the yoke or pocket with satin ribbon or broderie anglaise lace.

NOTE If a padded effect is required, insert a piece of polyester batting (wadding) between the appliquéd yoke and the lining and quilt around the outline of the figure with tiny running stitches (see Textile Sandwich on page 40).

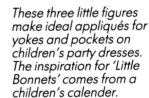

These three little figures make ideal appliqués for yokes and pockets on children's party dresses. The inspiration for 'Little Bonnets' comes from a children's calender.

This bright design provides the perfect opportunity to use up old scraps of piped bias binding, cord and eyelets. It is an ideal motif for a tracksuit top.

YELLOW HEART TENNIS SHOES

Materials
25 cm of sprigged fabric (see also candy stripe plimsolls on page 12)
Small piece of white cotton for toe-cap
1 card of striped, piped bias binding
50 cm of yellow cord for laces
9 white eyelets
Yellow machine thread
Iron-on vilene

Template (page 161)

1. Enlarge the template to the required size by following the instructions on page 12.

2. Using the Direct Appliqué Technique on page 18, transfer the design onto the vilene and then onto the fabric. Cut a complete pair of sprigged plimsolls and then superimpose the white toe-caps and soles.

3. Tack the piped bias binding in position using the photograph as your guide.

4. Position the design on the garment and machine satin stitch all the details and raw edges (a zipper foot is ideal for the satin stitching next to the piped bias binding).

5. Insert nine white eyelets and thread the cord through them. Tie the laces and secure the knot with a few back stitches.

BEADED POCKET

Materials
Cream material for the pocket background
A selection of African beads for the fringe
A selection of matching embroidery thread
  for the woven section and the animal
4 pearl buttons
A bead needle
White machine thread
Iron-on vilene

Stitches (pages 26-33)
French knots

Template (page 166)

1. Trace the design onto the iron-on vilene, shiny side up. Iron it onto the wrong side of the pocket fabric and cut out the pocket leaving a 2 cm seam allowance all around the outer edge of the pocket.

2. Hold the pocket up to the light and lightly pencil the animal shape onto the right side of the fabric.

3. Embroider the animal and geometric shapes in French knots using three strands of embroidery thread, and weave the border design using four strands of embroidery thread (the weft in one colour and the warp in another – see page 33).

4. Begin the beadwork just below the woven border. Use a double thread and begin with a knot and a back stitch. Exit below the weaving; string the colour combination onto your thread using the photograph as your guide. Turn back and push the needle through all the beads except the last bead of the design (this bead holds the dangling string together). End off each string individually with a strong back stitch.

5. To finish off the pocket, turn the top seam allowance under to form a hem. Fold the seam allowance under on the other three sides and hand hem the pocket onto your garment. Decorate the four corners with pearl buttons.

The inspiration for this beaded pocket was an African beaded amulet from the Mfengu tribe. The original design was made entirely of beads but I have adapted the idea and combined fabric, beadwork and embroidery for a more practical pocket.

*C*hildren's party hats from the Far East were the inspiration for these delightful circus creatures. Take a basic long- or short-sleeved T-shirt and add an animal appliqué – a squirrel, elephant, lion and tiger, panda or zebra.

These animals are made using the Double Vilene Technique (page 20) and basic embroidery stitches (pages 26-33). The templates can be found on pages 131-136.

91

*B*ears have always been a firm favourite. These bears are so versatile they can be scaled down for tiny tots or enlarged for adult impact. Your choice of fabric will dictate the mood.

TARTAN SCARF TEDDY

Materials
30 cm of fabric suitable for a teddy (i.e. towelling, velour or velvet)
Two strips of tartan fabric 30 x 10 cm for his scarf
Small pieces of tartan for the cap
A tiny button
Matching machine thread
50 cm of iron-on vilene
Brown, black and white embroidery thread for the details (or a selection of beads if you prefer beaded details)

Stitches (pages 26-33)
Buttonhole stitch, French knots, bullion knots, Roumanian stitch

Template (pages 123-125)

1. With the shiny side up, trace the teddy onto the iron-on vilene using a soft pencil.

2. For the contrast as seen in the black velvet bear or cream velour bear, trace the paws and nose separately onto the vilene. Cut out the pieces on the pencil outlines.

3. Iron the vilene, shiny side down, onto the wrong side of the fabric. Cut out the vilene-backed fabric pieces.

4. Tack the nose and paws in place onto the teddy (black velvet or cream velour bears).

5. Place the prepared appliqué onto a larger piece of vilene, shiny side away from the design. Be sure that the second piece of vilene protrudes all round the design.

6. Satin stitch all the details and raw edges of the design. (Machine setting: zigzag,

A child's toy is the inspiration for this sketch of a teddy bear by a 14-year-old art student. The black velvet bear is a sophisticated adult interpretation for an appliqué.

Lace, ribbon and bows are such fun for a pair of bears in tutus and ballet pumps.

width of approx. 2 and closeness of approx. ½.) Always work from the centre outwards.

7. Cut away the excess vilene.

8. Embroider or bead the eyes and nose. To embroider the eyes use a combination of long and short buttonhole stitch filled with one white French knot and two black bullion knots. Embroider the nose in black Roumanian stitch. To bead the eyes, sew on large sequins attached with tiny seed beads and couch the nose with seed beads by stringing a number of tiny beads onto the thread and then catching the thread down between every second bead.

9. For the scarf, cut two strips of tartan fabric 30 x 10 cm. Fold the strips in half lengthwise. With right sides facing, machine the long side and one short side of each strip.

10. Turn the strips through to the right side. Machine stitch the opening closed, about 3 cm from the end of the scarf. Pull the weft threads from the warp to make the fringe (fray). Hem the opposite short ends of the fabric to the teddy's neck and loop the two frayed ends to form a warm scarf.

11. For the cap, trace the three panels and the brim onto the vilene, shiny side up.

12. Cut out and iron the panel shapes onto the tartan, leaving a 2 cm seam allowance around each piece. Cut the brim double, leaving a 2 cm seam allowance around the vilene-backed shape.

13. Machine stitch the three panels together. With right sides together, stitch the outer edge of the brim, clip curves and turn through to the right side.

14. Tuck the raw edge of the cap into the open side of the brim and top stitch. Turn all the seam allowances under and top stitch the outer edge of the cap.

15. Cover a small button with tartan fabric and stitch it to the cap.

16. Attach the cap to the teddy by hand hemming or machine stitching it along the upper brim edge.

17. Attach the tartan teddy to your background by hand hemming or by machine straight stitching just inside the satin-stitched edge.

This bear has a more feminine touch. Use beige suede, a pink neck-tie and an embroidered posy for instant appeal. Fabric paint can be used to make up the face.

WOOLLEN CAT

Materials
Small balls of cream, beige and brown
  wool
Black, white, blue and brown embroidery
  thread
Brown nylon thread for whiskers
Cream, brown and beige machine thread
  for couching the wool in place
Iron-on vilene
A piece of floral print (suitable for floral
  cut-outs)
Matching machine thread
Yellow embroidery thread for flower
  centres

Stitches (pages 26-33)
Bullion rosebuds, French knots, extended
  French knots and back stitch

Template (page 123)

Embroider a woollen cat onto a toddler's outfit and add appliquéd flowers for that special party.

1. Trace the cat design onto the vilene, shiny side down. Cut out on the lines and iron the vilene shape onto your garment.

2. Back stitch the outlines of the cat in a fine brown wool. Fill in the beige and cream areas in chunky wool using couching (see pages 26-33 on Embroidery).

3. Work a bullion rosebud eye, beginning with black then changing to blue and finishing with white.

4. French knot the whisker base and make whiskers using a double strand of nylon thread. Enter from the right side of the design and make a back stitch into the French knot leaving a small end protruding. Exit again on the top side and cut the nylon leaving a small extension.

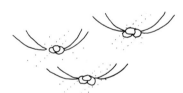

5. Cut out the flower designs from the floral material, tack them onto the background and machine satin stitch the raw edges. Work French knots and extended French knots in the floral centres using three strands of yellow embroidery thread.

TARTAN CAT

Materials
A small piece of tartan fabric
25 cm black velvet ribbon
A tiny piece of black chintz for the nose
Black and red machine thread
Black and white embroidery thread
Brown nylon thread for the whiskers
Iron-on vilene

Stitches (pages 26-33)
Buttonhole bars, stab stitch, French knots

Template (page 122)

1. Enlarge or reduce the design to suit the garment by following the instructions on page 12.

2. Make the cat appliqué by following the instructions for the Double Vilene Technique on page 20.

3. Machine satin stitch all the details and the raw edges, remembering to stitch about 1 cm inside the edge from just below the ear to the neck. This small area of fabric can be frayed to give a 'cheeky' finish.

4. Embroider the eyes in black buttonhole bars and white stab stitch eyelashes. French knot the nose.

5. Using double nylon thread, make the whiskers: enter the fabric from the right side, leaving a small end of nylon protruding. Now make a back stitch and exit again on the right side. Cut off the nylon thread with 2 cm protruding.

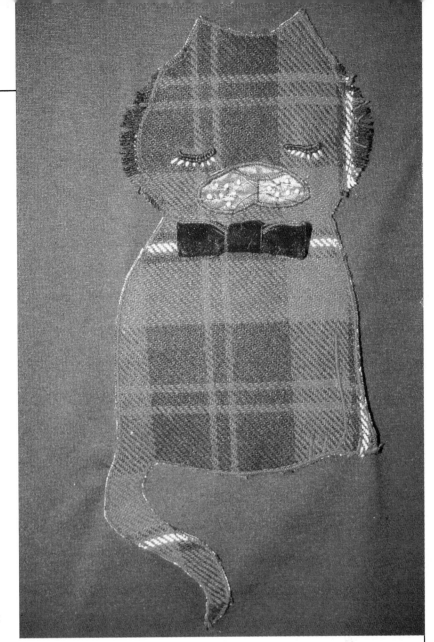

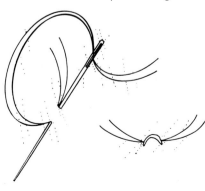

6. Make the black velvet ribbon into a bow tie: join the two ends together as shown below. Wrap another small band of ribbon around the middle of the bow tie and hand hem at the back of the bow. Stitch the bow to the cat's neck.

This rather refined fellow looks terrific on a simple T-shirt. He would also look delightful on a pullover teamed up with tartan knickerbockers for the younger set.

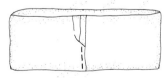

7. Machine straight stitch the completed appliqué to your garment.

*F*or an author and designer, the joy of sharing creative ideas can be diminished by giving the exact colours and quantities of fabric used, so I have devoted the following pages to a feast of imaginative and inspiring concepts using different media. Often the source material or preliminary art work has been included to illustrate how an idea grew into a creative appliqué statement.

The soft sculptured face, and pyramid of beads for her dress make a charming miniature on a child's outfit.

These 'autumn abstracts' were inspired by the wonderful wall-paintings seen on the houses of the Ndebele tribe. Imagine the design repeated horizontally along the border of a cream linen skirt or used vertically as a panel in a jacket.

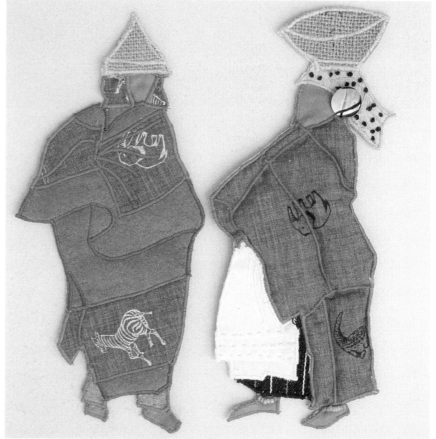

A double vilene appliqué in hessian, denim and felt. The shapes are lightly quilted and finished with a touch of beadwork.

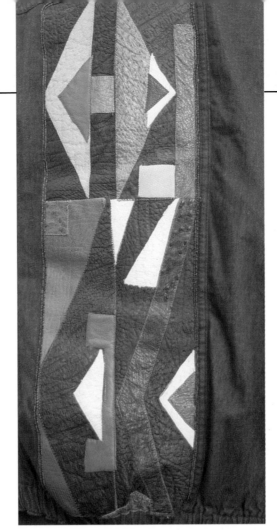

Ostrich skin in exciting colours makes an unusual geometric panel on a blue denim jacket.

This design is embroidered onto a piece of green hessian. Soft sculpture is used for the face, arms and legs and silk coils for the hair.

The stark, simple lines of the mud house are decorated with joyous colours and exciting geometrics. The appliqué shows the three-dimensional house with a two-dimensional pattern. The third dimension is suggested by the receding lines of the side wall.

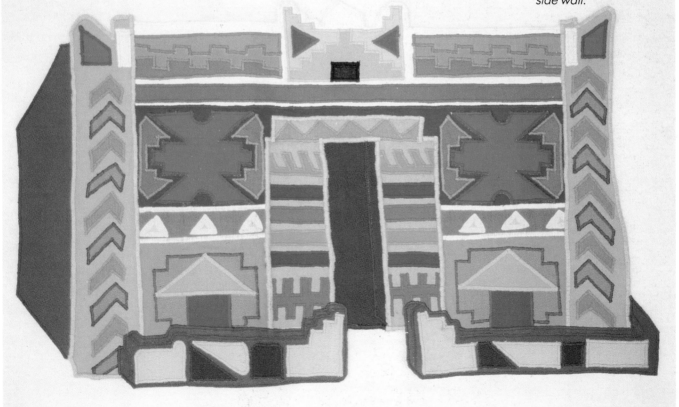

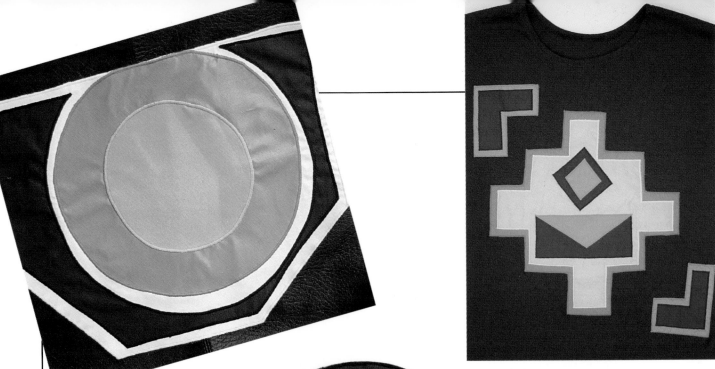

A strong, diagonal, African-inspired design is both striking and slimming.

The suggestion of feathers is created by the use of patterned linens, which have been superimposed on basic black. The centres of the piercing red eyes are decorated with rhinestones.

These striking succulent flora translate extremely well into appliqué. A change in the colour of the leaves is achieved by altering the direction of the velvet pile. The black background absorbs the shapes while the white background provides a striking contrast.

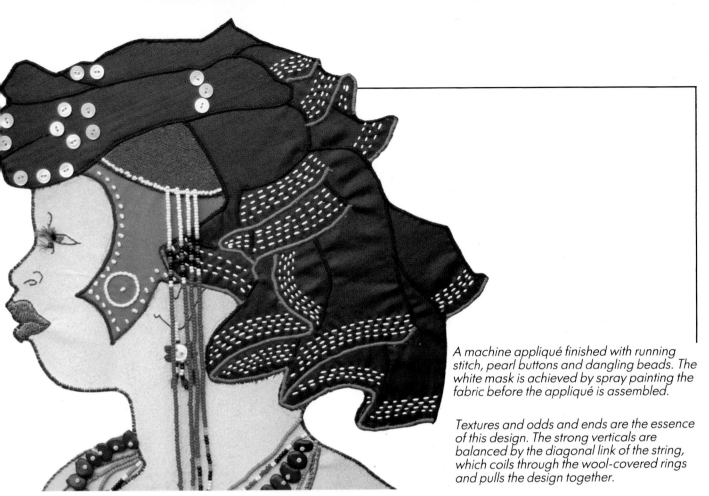

A machine appliqué finished with running stitch, pearl buttons and dangling beads. The white mask is achieved by spray painting the fabric before the appliqué is assembled.

Textures and odds and ends are the essence of this design. The strong verticals are balanced by the diagonal link of the string, which coils through the wool-covered rings and pulls the design together.

The appliqué has been fully overlocked and is ready to be attached to a sophisticated outfit.

The free-standing petals are made using the double fabric technique. Notice the attractive attention to detail in the stamens.

This dramatic craypas (oil pastel) artwork made by a teenage art student was the source of the inspiration for the glazed cotton poinsettia appliqué.

The double vilene technique in progress.

Notice the different handling of the petals - double fabric appliqué and free-form petals are highlighted with embroidery details.

A wonderful abstraction of proteas and lilies by Melissa Schnaid, a young art pupil. An exciting design to interpret in fabric.

The appliqué petals are given extra impact with bold stab stitch. The stamens are buttonhole bars finished with bullion knots, and anchored with knots and extended French knots.

A stunning floral appliqué on the front panel of a raw silk jacket.

Tiger lilies, amaryllis, rhododendrons and St Joseph's lilies in appliqué abundance.

White chintz blooms and green batik leaves.

Exquisitely embroidered dusty pink blooms with olive green heavily embroidered leaves are appliquéd onto a hand-knitted garter stitch top.

Colourful bullion knot rosebushes to brighten a yoke.

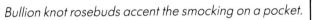

Bullion knot rosebuds accent the smocking on a pocket.

The pre-printed fabric shapes are accented with machine appliqué outlines and hand-embroidered centres.

Brighten up a pocket or yoke with this tiny basket of flowers. The flowers are a combination of bullion and French knots while the basket weave is created by the use of buttonhole bars and bullion knots.

A direct appliqué given incredible life with three-dimensional petals pinched at the tips and embroidered in position with extended French knots.

A striking appliqué of hibiscus with golden spider's web, French knot and extended French knot centres.

Artistic licence comes into play with this multi-coloured neckline. The double fabric appliqué flowers are attached to the garment by satin stitching along the outer edge of the design.

The back yoke of this jacket features lilies while the front yoke provides a total contrast with a pair of ladybirds.

An old-fashioned country flower, the nasturtium, adds a splash of colour to a top and skirt. Notice the scale change from the skirt to the top - the design has been reduced or enlarged to suit the application. The double fabric appliqué nasturtiums have been cut out to create a shaped border and interesting eyelet effect.

This delightful design on a pocket was inspired by a birthday greetings card. Simple appliqué combines successfully with hand-embroidered details.

A greetings card was the inspiration for this hand appliquéd design with three-dimensional appeal.

Inspired by a greetings card, the basic design was first appliquéd and then embellished with glorious needlework. The mouse is 'thumb' size.

Delightful appliqués for children's dungarees.

A simple appliqué with a humorous touch in the addition of earrings, wool hair and pleated skirt.

A mixed media collage by Melissa Schnaid, a 14-year-old art student from Les Design Studio.

The shiny silky hair is made from coils of silk couched into the appliqué. The faces and figures are lightly padded and finished with embroidery, lace and pearls.

Designed and created by Sheryl Stein, a 16-year-old art student from Les Design Studio, this graphic has been sensitively translated into a fabric collage of mixed media.

These photographs show the frivolous and flamboyant ideas of the young final-year designers from Leggats Academy of Design.

Prizewinner of the 1988 Woolmark Competition, Monica Song, designed this stunning outfit complete with black, pure wool trapunto quilting, piped braiding and hand-covered fasteners.

The trouser fabric is repeated on the midrif top in the form of an appliqué design.

Heavy white velvet is caught in bow-like bunches with beaded pearl clusters.

Yellow Dior roses trimmed with magenta binding accent the legs and neckline of this outfit.

CREATIVE APPLIQUÉ

A cascade of Dior roses lifts a youthful boob-tube top and stretch miniskirt.

Appliquéd panels form the irregular hemline of this 20's-style evening dress. The matching silk hip band is finished with a Dior rose.

Black embroidered net sets off a satin mini two-piece.

3 TEMPLATES AND PATTERNS

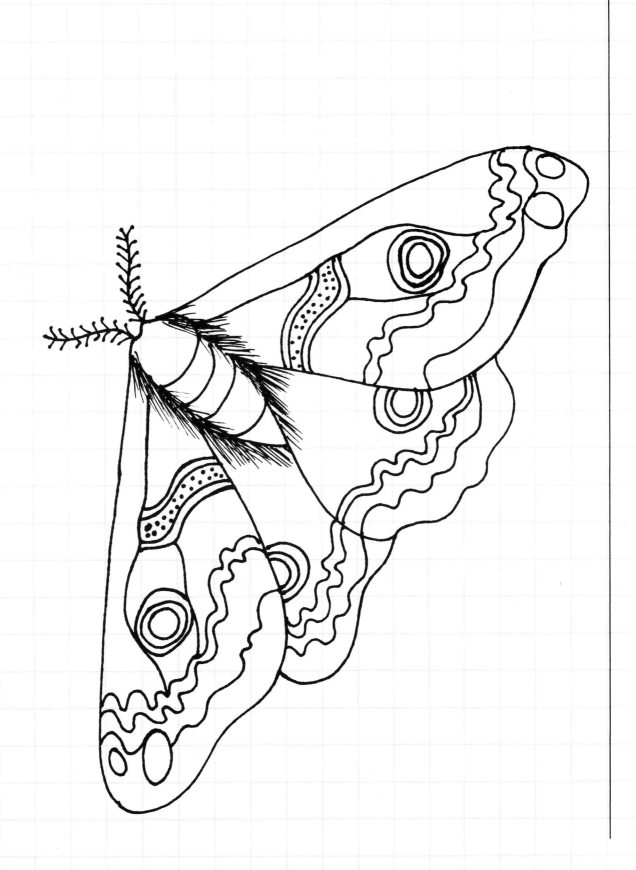

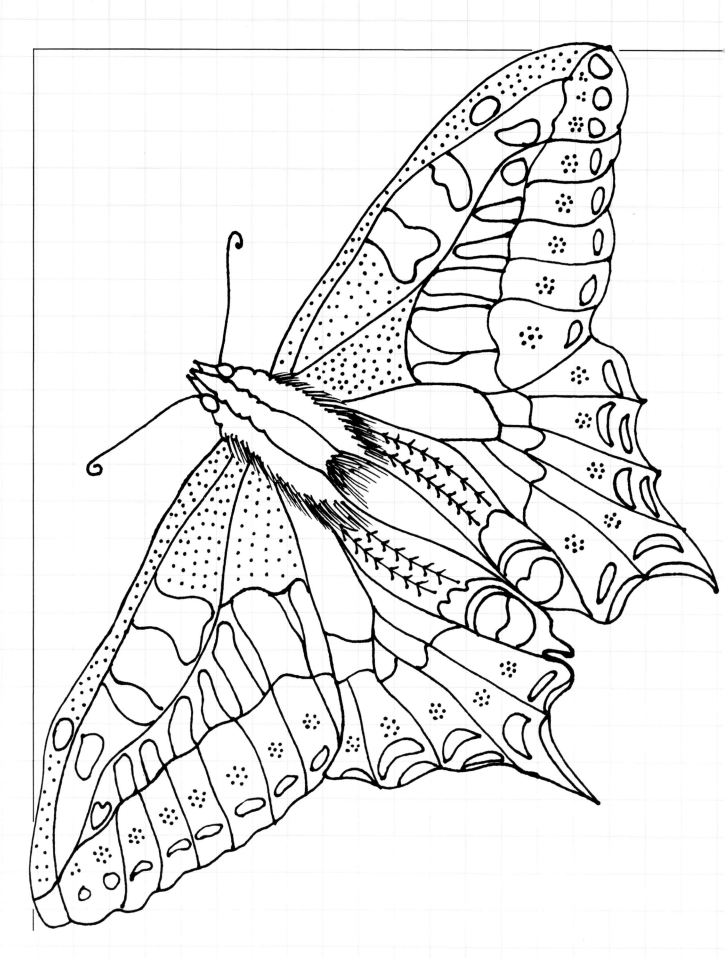

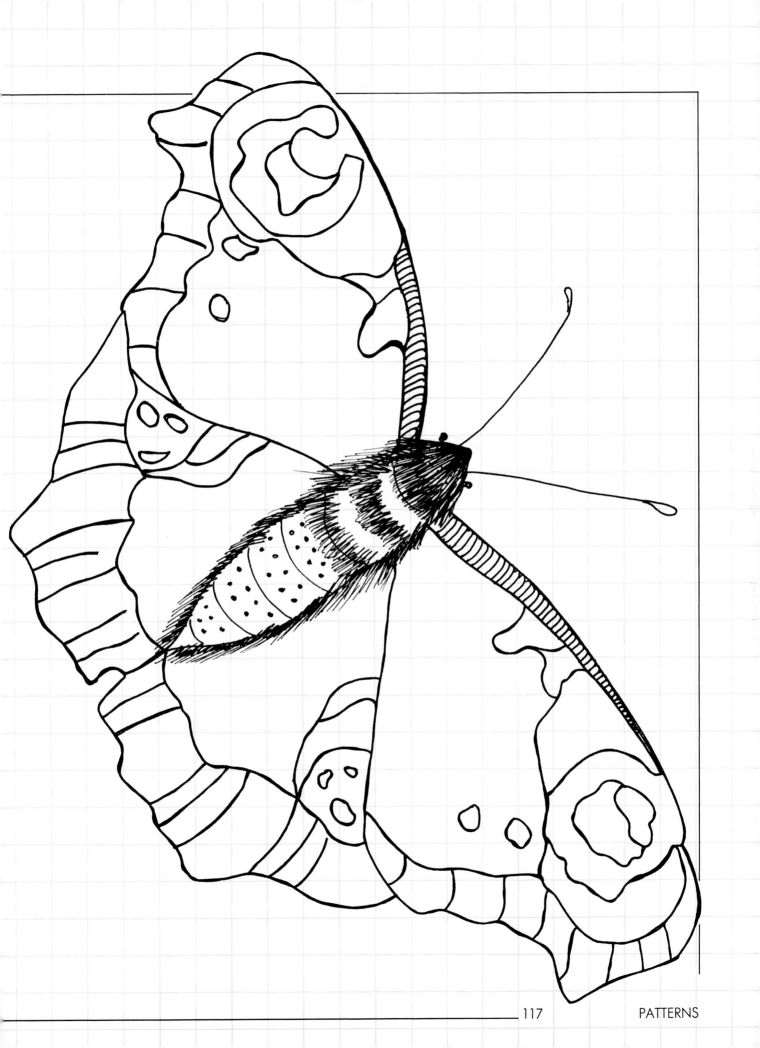

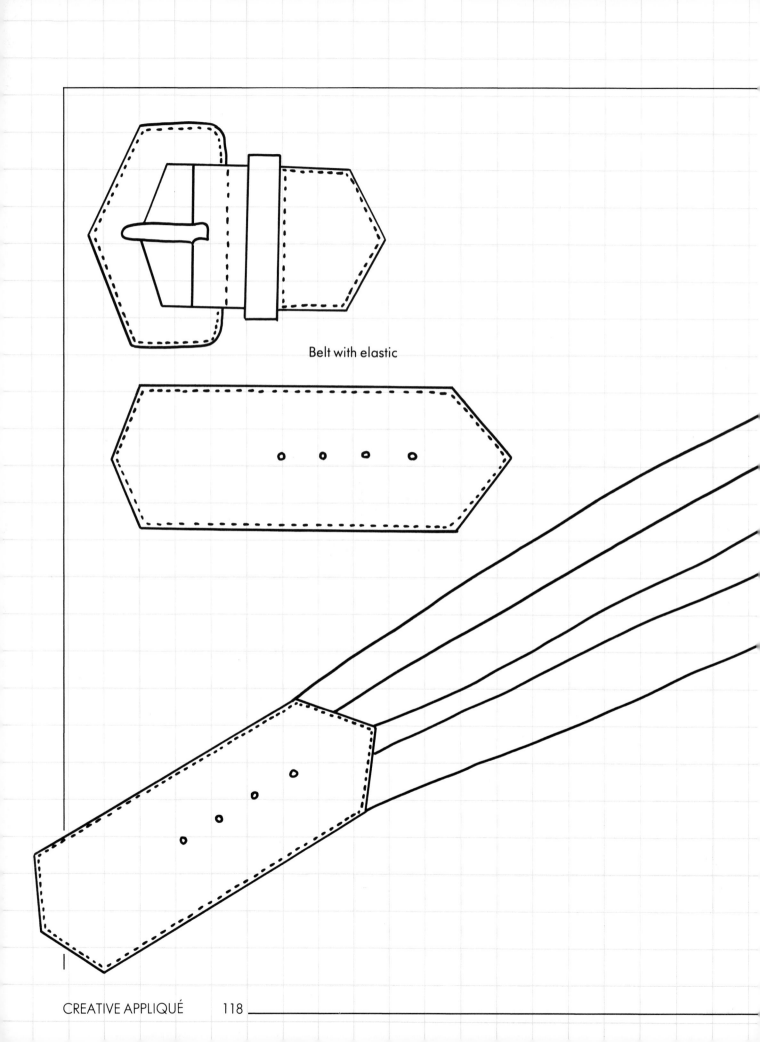

Belt with elastic

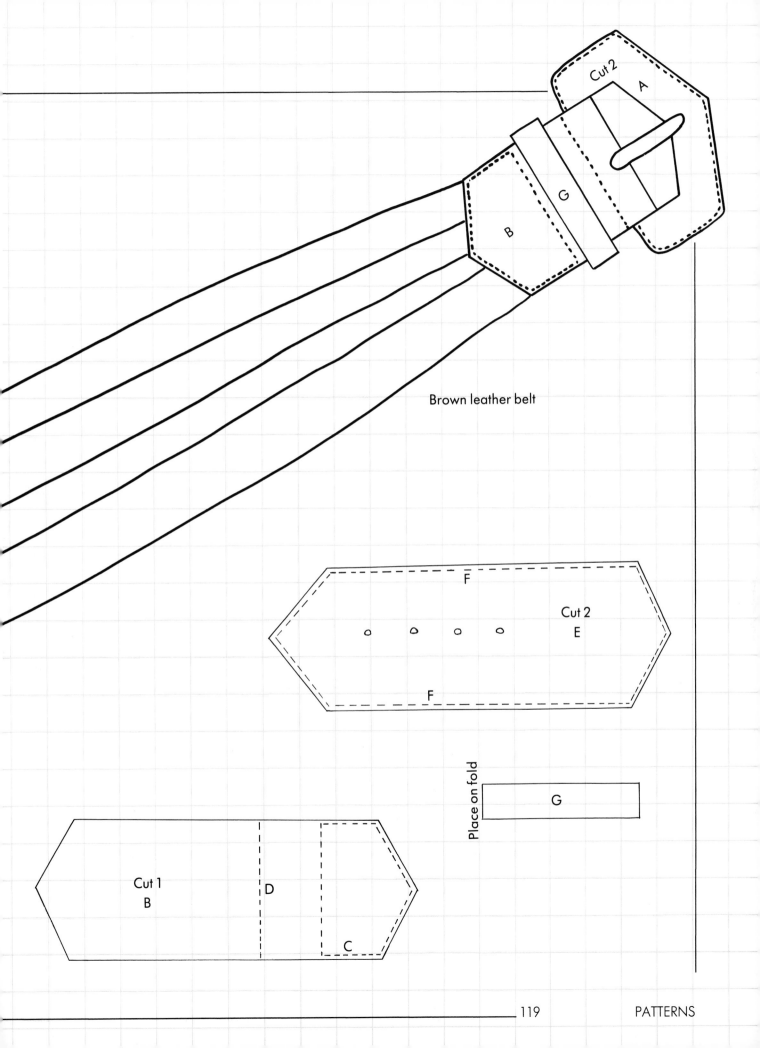

Cut 2

A

G

B

Brown leather belt

F

Cut 2
E

F

Place on fold

G

Cut 1
B

D

C

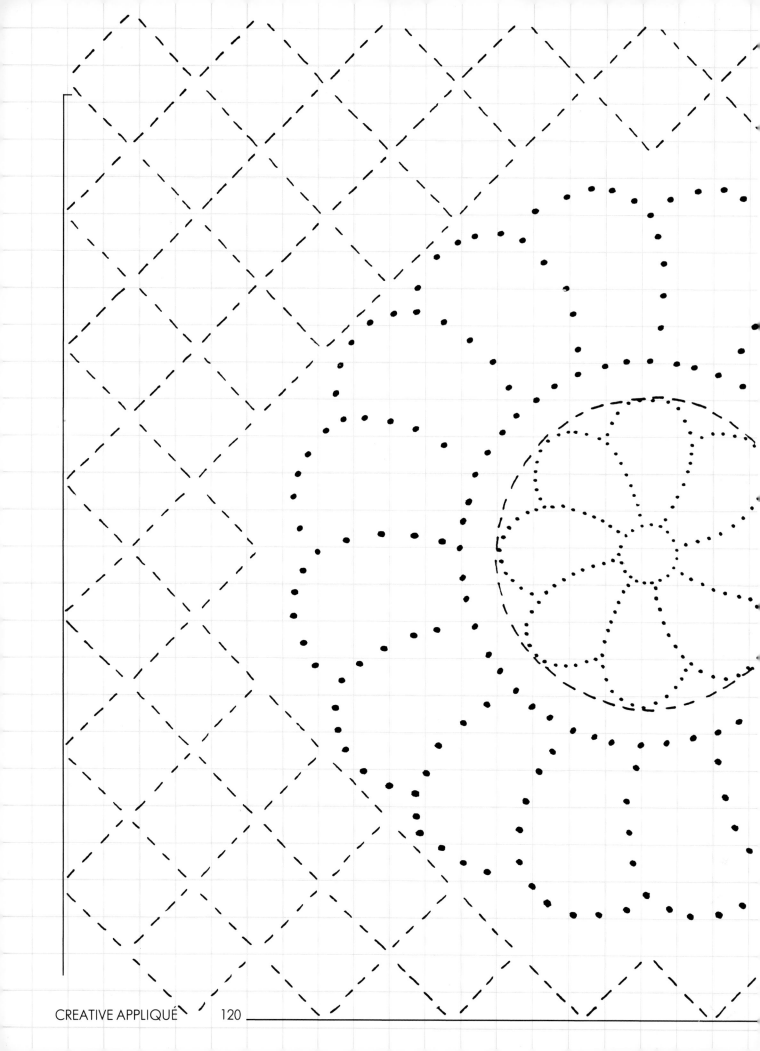

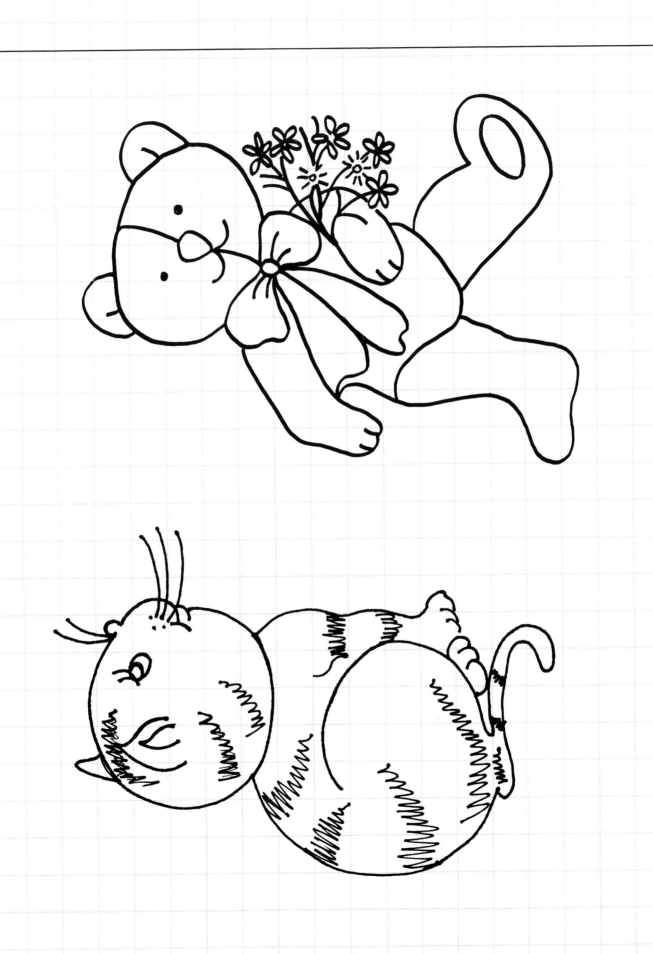

PATTERNS

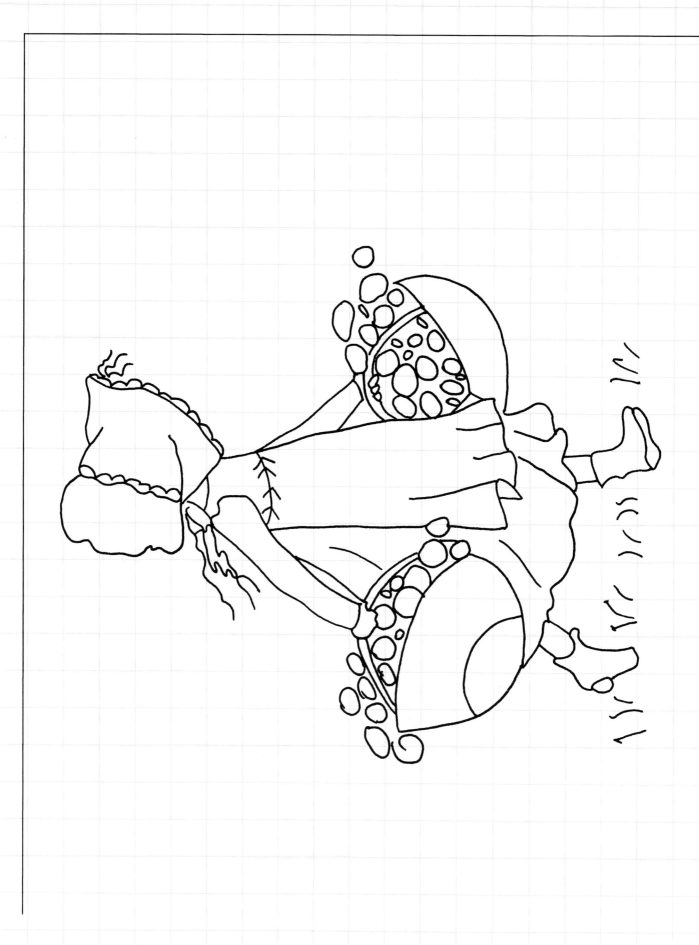

PATTERNS

PATTERNS

139

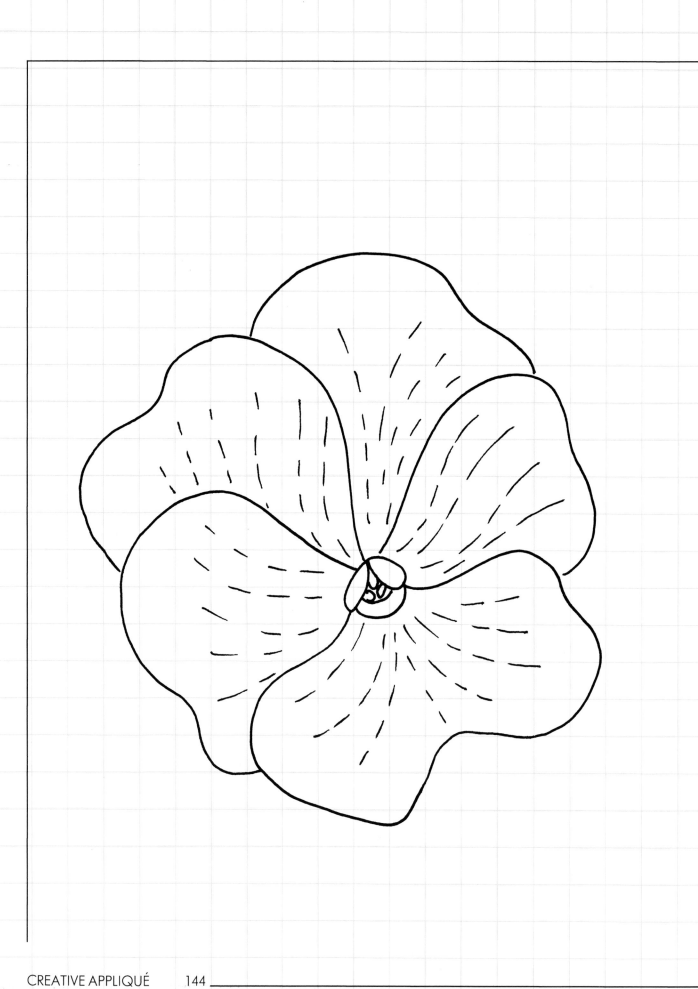

PATTERNS

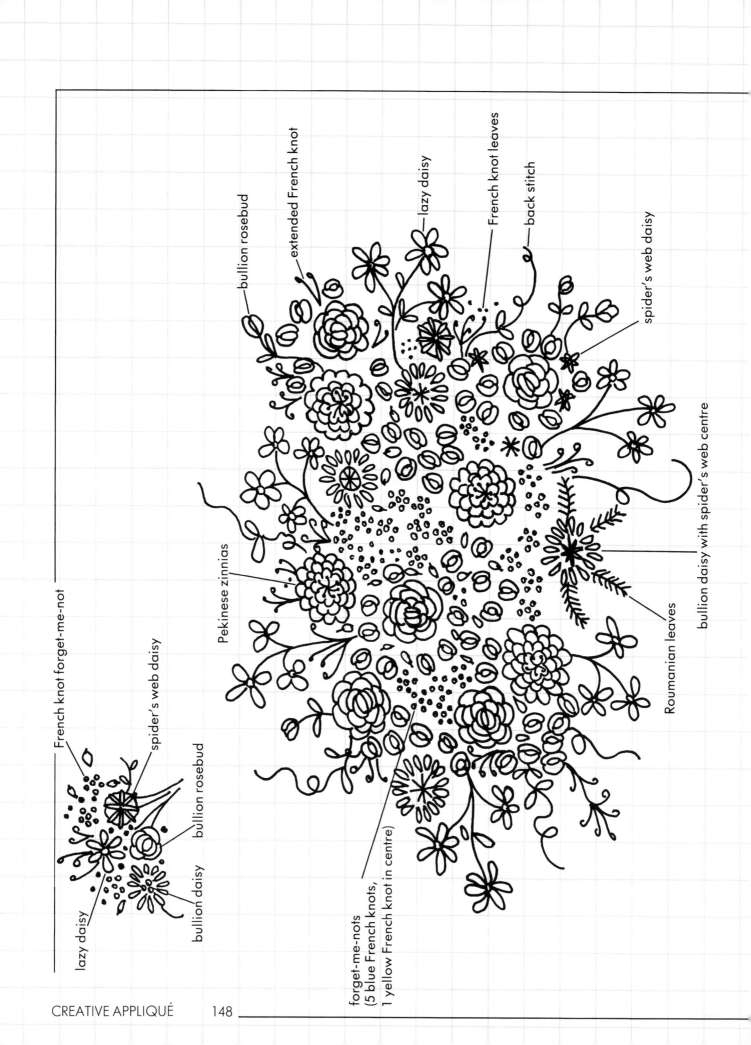

bullion rosebud

extended French knot

lazy daisy

French knot leaves

back stitch

spider's web daisy

bullion daisy with spider's web centre

Roumanian leaves

Pekinese zinnias

forget-me-nots
(5 blue French knots,
1 yellow French knot in centre)

French knot forget-me-not

spider's web daisy

bullion rosebud

bullion daisy

bullion daisy

lazy daisy

PATTERNS

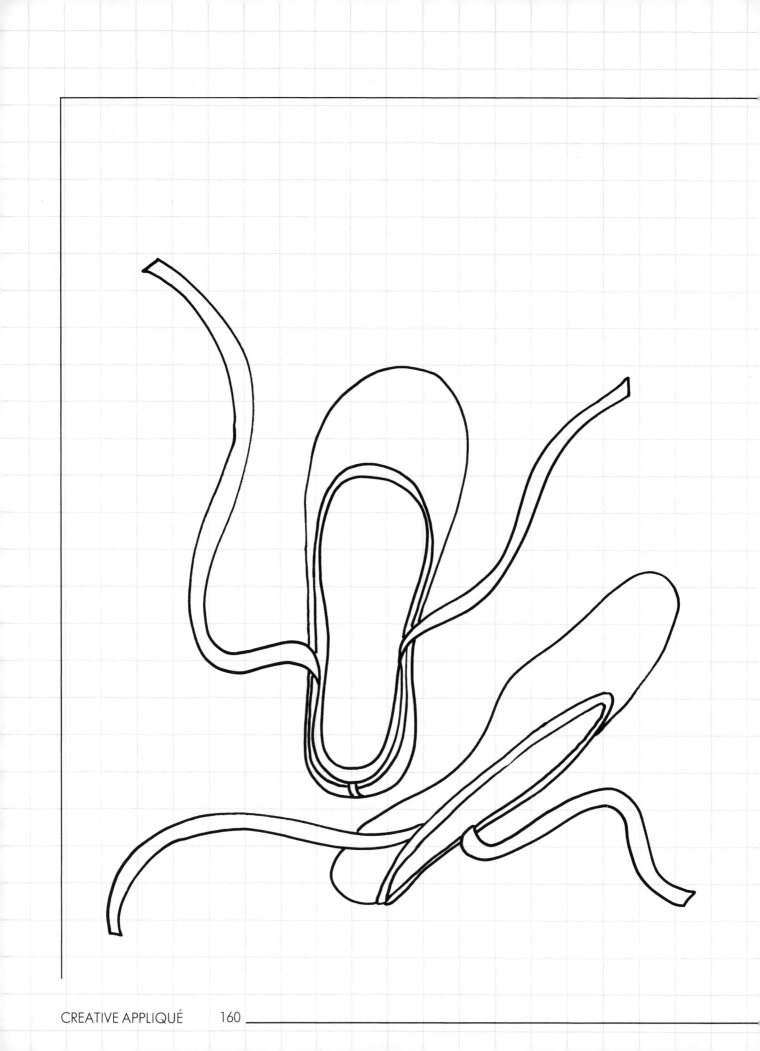

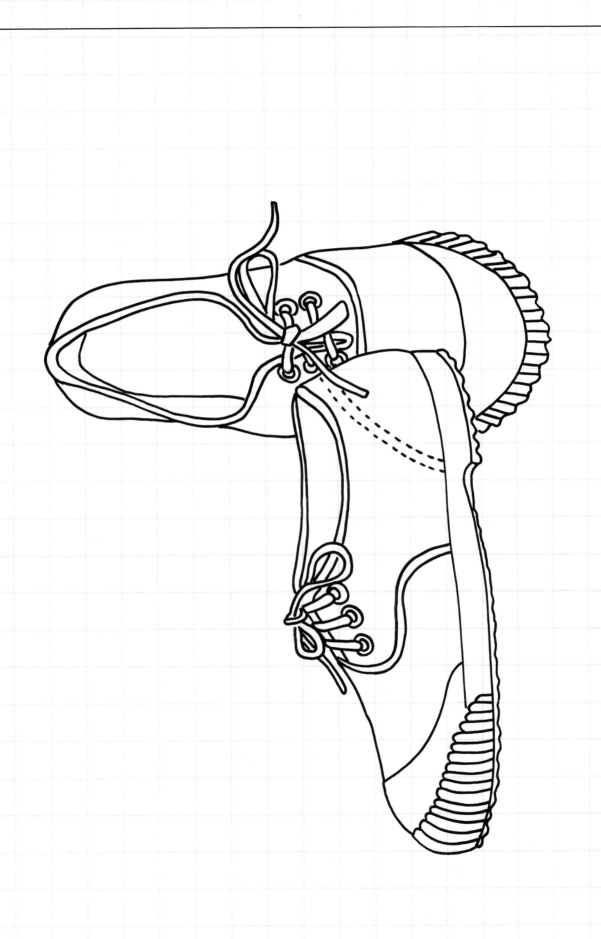

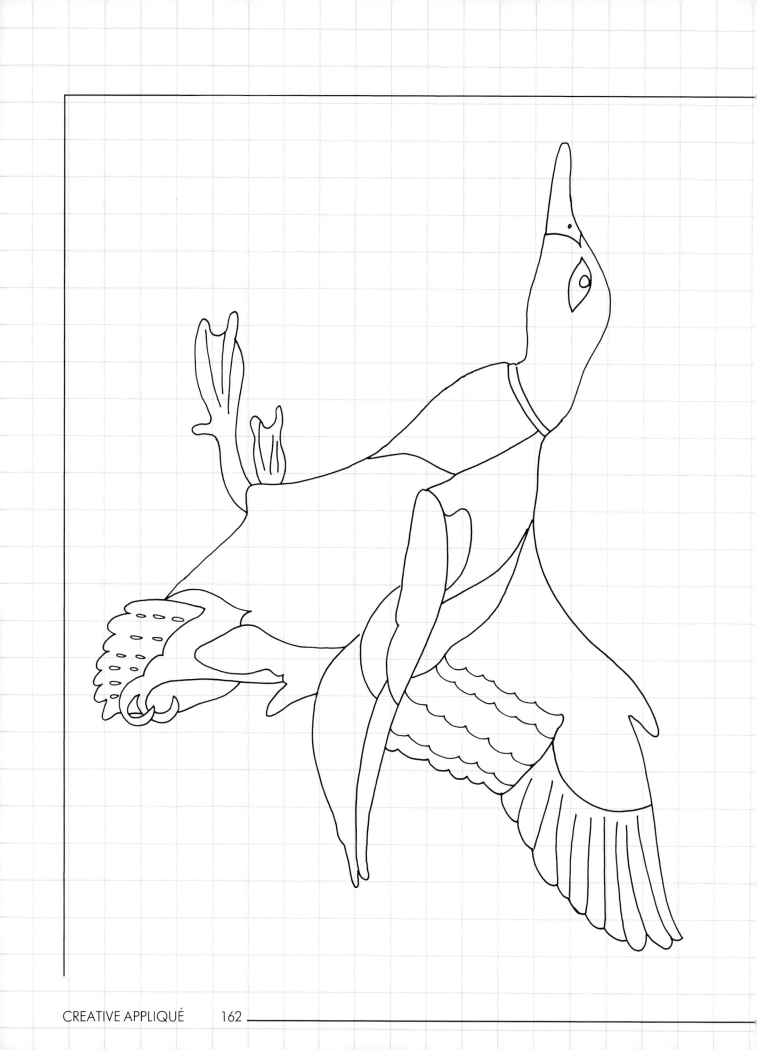

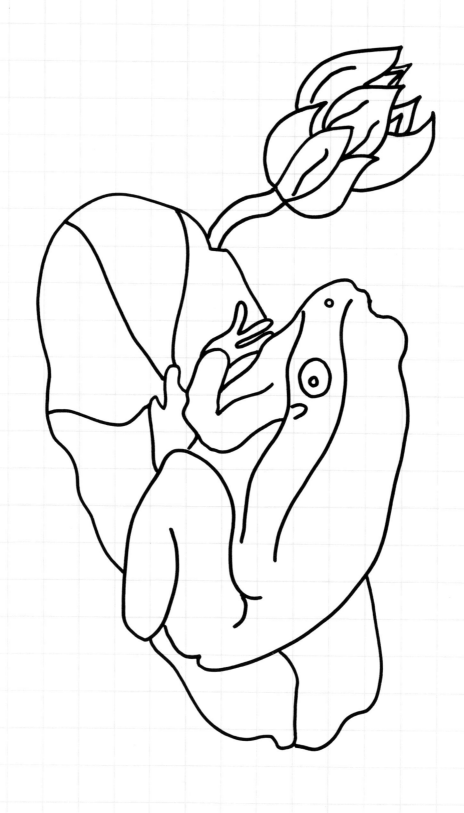

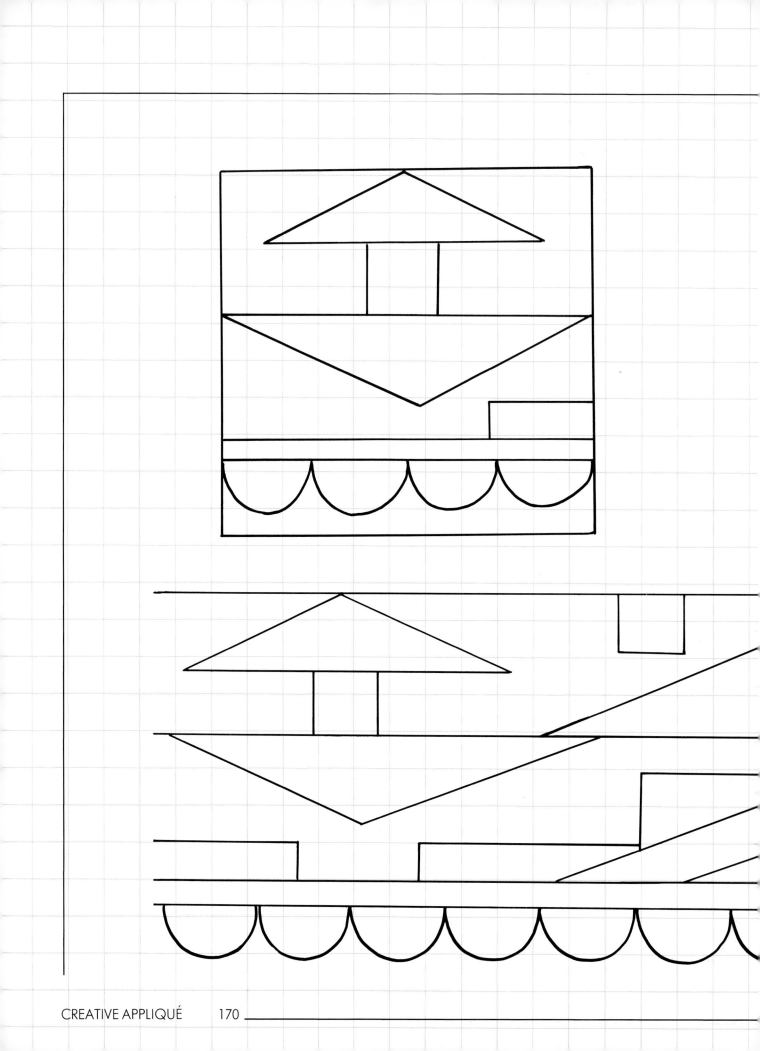

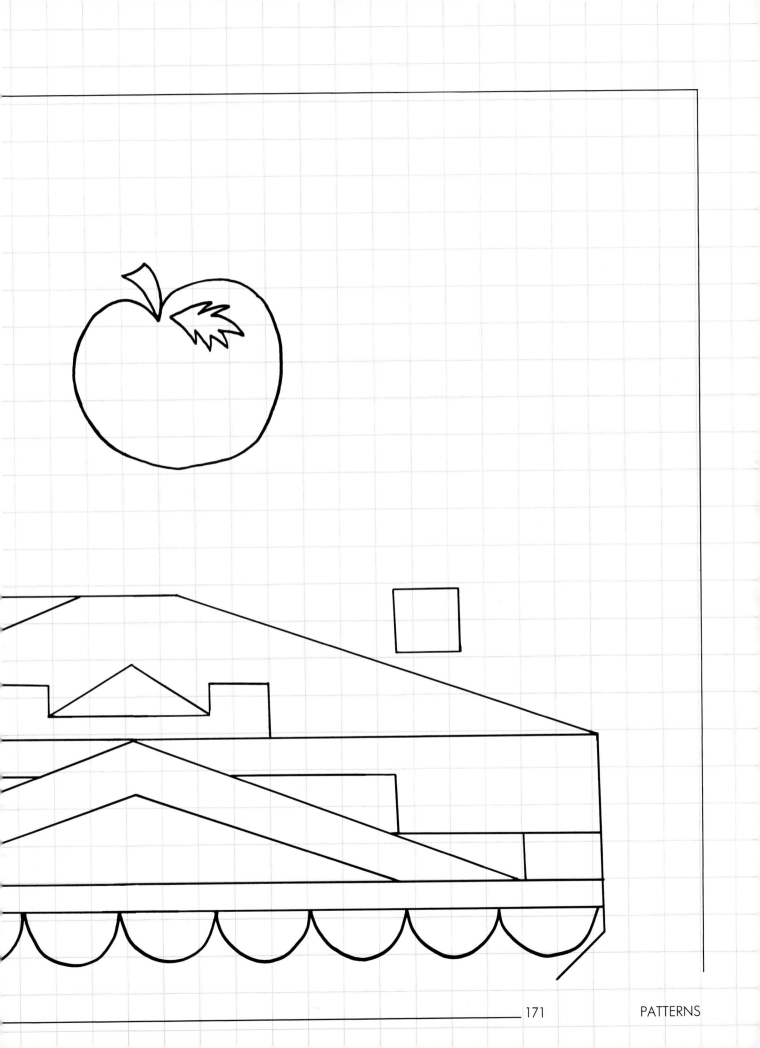

Place on fold

Cut 2

INDEX